HOSPITAL
ARCHITECTURE + DESIGN

MASTERPIECES

CHRISTINE NICKL-WELLER | HANS NICKL (EDS.)

HOSPITAL
ARCHITECTURE + DESIGN

BRAUN

PREFACE. VORWORT. PRÉFACE.

In planning new hospital buildings, innovations in the healthcare sector such as the combination of design and wellness are combined with economic and medical trends. High stylistic and functional demands combined with contemporary design also set new benchmarks for healing and care buildings. The term "hospital architecture" actually incorporates a wide range of functional buildings – from small basic care hospitals, via specialized clinics and up to large-scale hospitals offering maximum care, such as university hospitals.

Masterpieces Hospital Architecture + Design provides a comprehensive international overview of current hospital projects. Hospital buildings are among the most complex, and thus the most interesting, construction projects. They are particularly demanding because there usually is a long time span between the initial idea and the occupancy of a new building. At the same time, current political, social, technical and medical changes have to be always taken into account.

Without exceptions, the presented examples of new buildings show a high degree of artistic design and convey consistency. Sustainable construction is a must for hospital architecture, since changes in the medical sector take place very rapidly. In addition,

Innovationen im Gesundheitswesen wie die Verbindung von Design und Wohlbefinden werden bei der Planung neuer Krankenhausbauten in Relation zu ökonomischen und medizinischen Trends gesetzt. Ein hoher Anspruch an Ausgestaltung und Funktionalität in Kombination mit zeitgenössischem Design setzt auch in den Heil- und Pflegebauten neue Maßstäbe.

Der Begriff „Krankenhausarchitektur" umschließt somit ein weites Spektrum an Aufgaben – angefangen bei kleinen Krankenhäusern der Grundversorgung über Fachkliniken bis hin zu den Großkliniken der Maximalversorgung wozu auch Universitätskliniken zählen. *Masterpieces Hospital Architecture + Design* gibt einen umfassenden und internationalen Überblick über aktuelle Projekte des Krankenhausbaus. Krankenhausbauten gehören zu den komplexesten, damit aber auch zu den interessantesten Bauaufgaben. Anspruchsvoll besonders deshalb, weil zwischen der ersten Idee und dem Bezug eines neuen Hauses häufig ein sehr langer Zeitraum liegt. Laufend sind aktuelle politische, gesellschaftliche, technische sowie medizinische Veränderungen zu berücksichtigen.

Die präsentierten Neubaubeispiele zeigen ausnahmslos ein hohes gestalterisches Niveau und stehen für Beständigkeit. Nachhaltiges Bauen ist für die Krankenhausarchitektur unumgänglich, weil sich die

Les hôpitaux modernes doivent tenir compte non seulement des facteurs économiques et des dernières découvertes médicales, mais aussi des tendances novatrices telles que l'importance du design dans les processus de guérison. De nouvelles exigences en matière de fonctionnalité et de modernisme apparaissent ainsi dans le secteur hospitalier.

Le terme « architecture hospitalière » concerne un vaste ensemble de réalisations, allant des petites unités locales aux CHU polyvalents, en passant par les cliniques spécialisées. Le présent ouvrage offre un panorama complet de cette spécialité architecturale au niveau international. Les hôpitaux comptent parmi les bâtiments les plus complexes de nos sociétés — et donc parmi les plus intéressants. Leur complexité est telle qu'un temps particulièrement long s'écoule souvent entre la genèse de l'idée et l'emménagement dans les nouveaux locaux. Ce qui requiert d'adapter constamment le projet à l'évolution du contexte politique, social, technique et bien entendu médical.

Toutes les réalisations présentées ici se caractérisent par l'excellence de leur design, leur capacité à suivre l'évolution très rapide des techniques médicales, et leur compatibilité avec une éventuelle utilisation pluridisciplinaire ultérieure. Des édifices

the basic structures of the building must be designed for interdisciplinary use to allow various uses. Hospital buildings designed this way and based on such planning consciously create constructive and artistic values that endure for centuries and inspire new architecture projects.

The holistic picture, which is the basis of hospital architecture, is not confined to "beautiful architecture", but rather practices modern construction as part of the responsible handling of natural resources.

The extension and expansion buildings contribute to the integration of the existing hospital into the local city or campus. In addition to functionality and architectural expression, they present a contemporary answer to the question of the presence of the hospital in the urban setting. Similar to any other craft or art, hospital architecture is in specific need for innovations. These must be applied in a targeted way where needed and must build on what was there before.

This book follows up on the success of *Hospital Architecture* – featuring the same high quality contents, this book focuses on international hospital architecture and new perspectives of sustainability and ecologic construction. All projects share the goal of fulfilling the requirements of hospitals as functional buildings, while meeting high esthetic demands. It is a form of architecture that contains all key design elements – the connection to the existing structures and location, the unity of technology and construction, the combination of design and room organization. All this takes place under the auspices of a special light. The same light that shines bright as one of the values that the health sector is all about – the light of hope.

Veränderungen im medizinischen Bereich sehr rasant vollziehen. Zudem müssen die Grundstrukturen des Gebäudes für die interdisziplinäre Nutzung angelegt sein, um Nutzungsänderungen zu ermöglichen. Außerdem schaffen so geplante Krankenhausbauten mit einem derartigen Planungshintergrund bewusst bauliche und künstlerische Werte, die Jahrzehnte überdauern und neue Architekturen inspirieren.

Das gesamtheitliche Bild, das die Krankenhausarchitektur begründet, beginnt und endet nicht bei „schöner Architektur", sondern praktiziert modernes Bauen als Teil des verantwortlichen Umgangs mit natürliche Ressourcen.

Die Erweiterungs- und Ergänzungsbauten leisten einen Beitrag zur Integration des bestehenden Krankenhauses in die Stadt oder in den Campus. Neben Fragen zu Funktionalität und dem architektonischen Ausdruck, muss eine zeitgemäße Antwort auf die Frage nach der Präsenz des Krankenhauses in der Stadt gefunden werden. Wie jedes andere Handwerk und jede andere Kunst verlangt ganz besonders die Krankenhausarchitektur nach Innovation. Diese muss gezielt dort eingesetzt werden, wo es ihrer bedarf und sie muss auf das bauen, was gewesen ist.

Der vorliegende Band knüpft an den Erfolg von *Hospital Architecture* an – angetreten mit demselben inhaltlichen Anspruch, wird der Fokus nun auf die internationale Krankenhausarchitektur gerichtet und es werden neue Perspektiven der Nachhaltigkeit und des ökologischen Bauens aufgezeigt. Allen Projekten gemeinsam ist selbstverständlich das Ziel, die funktionalen Anforderungen des Zweckbaus Krankenhaus zu erfüllen. Gleichzeitig werden sie den ästhetische Ansprüchen gerecht. Es ist eine Architektur, die alle wichtigen Entwurfselemente umfasst: den Bezug zum Bestehenden und zur Stadt, die Einheit von Technik und Konstruktion, die Verbindung von Gestaltung und Raumorganisation. All dies geschieht im Zeichen des Lichts. Es ist dasselbe Licht, das einen jener Werte darstellt, die dem Gesundheitswesen innewohnen: die Hoffnung.

qui répondent à un cahier des charges si exigeant vont assurément établir de nouvelles normes en matière de style et de technologie, et sont ainsi appelés à inspirer les architectes des décennies à venir.

Pour important qu'il soit, l'aspect esthétique n'est cependant pas la finalité de l'architecture hospitalière : celle-ci s'inscrit dans une conception moderne du BTP où la gestion responsable des ressources joue un rôle déterminant.

Les annexes nouvellement construites pour des établissements anciens contribuent à l'intégration de l'hôpital dans le tissu urbain. La tâche des architectes consiste dans ce cas à trouver une solution moderne aux problèmes posés par la présence d'un complexe hospitalier au cœur de la ville. Comme toute activité artistique, l'architecture hospitalière doit donc faire preuve de sa capacité à innover – et à développer des concepts compatibles avec les structures héritées du passé.

Le présent ouvrage s'inscrit dans la ligne du livre à succès Hospital Architecture. Il présente des réalisations internationales et met l'accent sur les perspectives que le développement durable et les méthodes de construction écologiques ouvrent à l'architecture hospitalière. Les nouveaux hôpitaux se veulent esthétiques, sans pour autant négliger les fonctions de base qui sont les leurs. Ils poursuivent en fait de multiples ambitions : s'intégrer à la ville et aux structures préexistantes, harmoniser technologie et architecture, satisfaire aux exigences en matière de design et d'organisation spatiale. Et surtout, ils accordent une importance capitale à l'éclairage, puisque la lumière incarne une valeur fondamentale des services de santé : l'espoir.

PROJECTS. PRO

JEKTE. PROJETS.

WOODBURY DERMATOLOGY CLINIC,
MEMPHIS, TN, USA

ARCHIMANIA

www.archimania.com
Client: Woodbury Dermatology Clinic, Completion: 2006, Gross floor area: 5,000 sq. ft., Photos: Jeffrey Jacobs Photography.

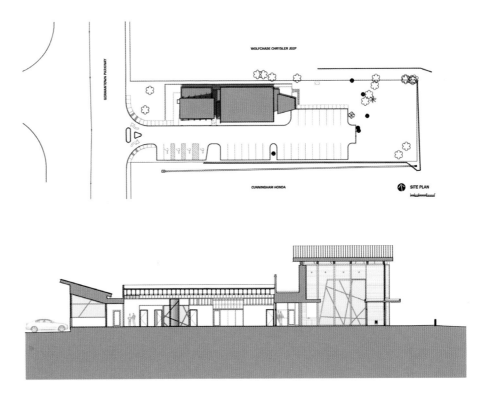

Left: Front façade. Links: Frontfassade. Gauche: Façade avant. | Right: Site plan and section. Rechts: Lageplan und Schnitt. Droite: Plan du site et coupe.

This accessible, retail-inspired dermatology clinic is invitingly warm and uniquely modern. The design makes a strong artistic statement in its mundane suburban context with four parts of the exterior composing the two functional components of the plan. The clinic is a simple and straightforward mass clad in custom stainless steel paneling, while the sloped glass and wood sculptural form contains the open, public waiting area. Stone and wood were chosen as building materials, while the resources and layout of the interior create a level of comfort and understanding internally and exteriorly.

Die leicht zugängliche, von einem Geschäft inspirierte dermatologische Klinik wirkt einladend und außergewöhnlich modern. Sie präsentiert eine deutlich künstlerische Aussage in ihrem Umfeld aus nüchternen Vorstadthäusern. Den äußeren vier Gebäudeelementen entsprechen die beiden funktionellen Komponenten des Grundrisses. Im einfachen mit speziell angefertigten Stahltafeln verkleideten Volumen ist die Klinik untergebracht. Die geneigte plastische Form aus Glas und Holz beherbergt den offenen Wartebereich. Als Baumaterialien kamen Stein und Holz zum Einsatz.

Cette clinique dermatologique d'accès facile se caractérise par son apparence à la fois chaleureuse et résolument moderne. Les quatre volumes formant deux unités fonctionnelles distinctes sont d'un style qui s'intègre parfaitement dans la banlieue chic où la clinique a été construite. À l'unité d'un style simple en panneaux d'acier inox réalisés sur mesure s'oppose l'unité en verre et bois d'une forme beaucoup plus sculpturale qui abrite les salles d'attente du public. Des matériaux tels que le bois et la pierre, associés à une décoration inspirée, créent une impression de confort et de sécurité tant à l'intérieur qu'à l'extérieur.

From left to right, from above to below:
Reception, hallway leading to patient rooms, interior.
Right: Glazed façade and wood cladding.

Von links nach rechts, von oben nach unten:
Empfang, Flur zu Patientenzimmern, Inneneinrichutng.
Rechts: Verglaste Fassade und Holzverkleidung.

De gauche à droite, de haut en bas:
Réception, couloir menant à la salle des patients, intérieur.
Droite: Façade en verre avec ossature en bois.

K-CLINIC,
NARA, JAPAN

ARCHITECTON AKIRA YONEDA

www.architecton.co.jp

Client: Koji Kawaguchi, **Completion:** 2007, **Gross floor area:** 199.43 m², **Photos:** Tomohiro Sakashita/ Tokyo,(c)Forward Stroke Inc./Tokyo.

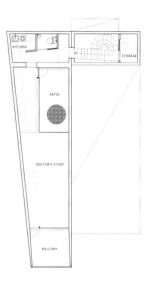

Left: Exterior. Links: Außenansicht. Gauche: Extérieur. | Right: Plan and site plan. Rechts: Grundriss und Lageplan. Droite: Plan et croquis du site.

K-Clinic is a small skin clinic built in a small town near Nara. It is made of steel-tube structure and located along the main street of the town. The surroundings used to be a gently-sloping hill. The cantilever of the upper floating part is maximal 17 meter long due to the "monocoque" structure that is composed of steel panel t6 and steel deck plate. The shape of the building basically reflects linearity and inclination of the road and suggests the missing profile of the land.

Die K-Clinic, eine kleine Hautklinik an der Hauptstraße einer Stadt bei Nara, ist von einer sanften Hügellandschaft umgeben. Ihre Stahlrohrkonstruktion mit „Schalen" aus T6-Stahlblechen und einer Stahldeckenplatte begrenzt die Auskragung des oberen schwebenden Teils auf maximal 17 Meter. Die Gebäudegestalt gibt im Wesentlichen die Geradlinigkeit und das Gefälle der Straße wieder und suggeriert nicht vorhandene Geländekonturen.

La « K-Clinic » est un petit édifice qui se dresse dans la rue principale d'une localité voisine de la ville de Nara. Elle se compose d'une structure monocoque en tube d'acier recouverte d'une enveloppe et construite sur un terrain en pente. La partie supérieure en cantilever, qui mesure dix-sept mètres de long à son extrémité, se compose de panneaux d'acier T6 et d'un toit également en acier. La forme linéaire du bâtiment s'adapte à l'inclinaison de la rue, tout en suggérant le profil de la colline sur lequel l'édifice a été construit.

From left to right, from above to below:
Exterior, patio, hallway with skylight, space with skylight.
Right: Gap between two volumes.

Von links nach rechts, von oben nach unten:
Außenansicht, Innenhof, Flur mit Oberlicht, Raum mit Oberlicht.
Rechts: Abstand zwischen zwei Baukörpern.

De gauche à droite, de haut en bas:
Extérieur, patio, couloir avec lucarne, espace avec lucarne.
Droite: Espace entre deux volumes.

MILDRED-SCHEEL HOUSE,
DRESDEN, GERMANY

BEHNISCH & PARTNER

www.behnisch.com

Client: Deutsche Krebshilfe e.V., Bonn for the University Clinical Center Carl Gustav Carus, **Completion:** 2002, **Gross floor area:** 32,172 sq. ft, **Photos:** Christian Kandzia.

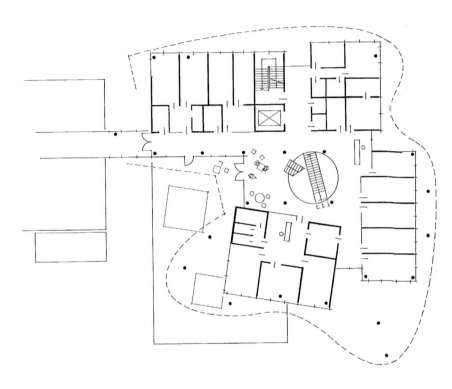

Left: Color designed façade. Links: Farbig gestaltete Fassade. Gauche: Façade en couleur. | Right: First floor plan. Rechts: Grundriss erste Etage. Droite: Plan du 1er étage.

The building's shape, interior layout, focus on light, openness and security, plants and colors all signify that it is a building designed for children. The functional areas are arranged orthogonally with administration and laboratories on the ground floor and the outpatient and day clinics on the first floor. The curved, sweeping second floor is a patient's ward with 12 rooms with individual styles and different geometric outlines that open onto a garden. The facility's core is an open hall, which connects all three levels and becomes increasingly lighter and freer to the top of the free formed stairs.

Die unprätentiöse Form des Baukörpers, seine innere Ordnung, Erlebniswerte wie Licht, Offenheit, Pflanzen und Farben spiegeln die Grundidee wider: Es ist ein Haus für Kinder. Die Funktionsbereiche sind orthogonal strukturiert. Verwaltung und Laborbereich befinden sich im Erdgeschoss, Ambulanz und Tagesklinik darüber. Das geschwungene und ausladende zweite Obergeschoss ist wesentlich freier gestaltet. Hier liegen 12 individuell zugeschnittene Patientenzimmer mit Blick auf einen Garten. Kern der Anlage ist eine offene Halle, die alle drei Nutzungsebenen verbindet und sich nach oben öffnet und lichtet.

La forme et les aménagements intérieurs ont été conçus en fonction de trois facteurs : lumière naturelle, aspect ouvert et sécurité. Les couleurs et les plantes choisies indiquent qu'il s'agit d'un bâtiment destiné aux enfants. Les différentes fonctions suivent un agencement orthogonal, avec les laboratoires et les bureaux au rez-de-chaussée, et les salles de soins pour patients externes au premier étage. Le second étage, construit sur un plan incurvé, abrite douze chambres qui donnent sur un jardin et ont toutes une forme et un style différents. Au centre de la clinique se trouve une grande cage d'escalier qui interconnecte les trois niveaux et devient de plus en plus clair vers le haut.

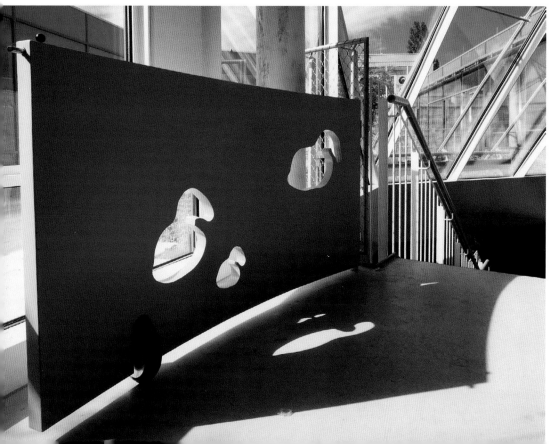

From left to right, from above to below:
Entrance, detail interior, staircase.
Right: View toward entrance.

Von links nach rechts, von oben nach unten:
Eingang, Interieurdetail, Treppenaufgang.
Rechts: Blick Richtung Eingang.

De gauche à droite, de haut en bas:
Entrée, détail de l'intérieur, escalier.
Droite: Vue sur l'entrée.

THE NEW MARTINI HOSPITAL,
GRONINGEN, THE NETHERLANDS

BURGER GRUNSTRA ARCHITECTEN ADVISEURS

www.burgergrunstra.nl
Client: Martini Ziekenhuis, **Completion:** 2007, **Gross floor area:** 58,000 m², **Photos:** Rob Hoekstra.

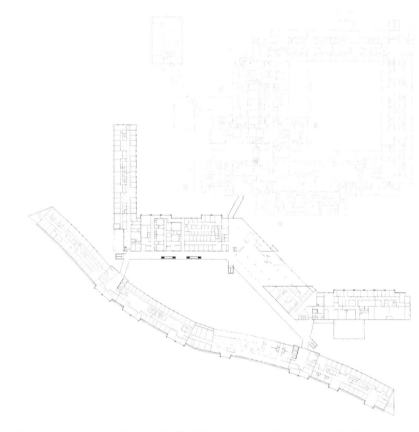

Left: Exterior view by night. Links: Außenansicht bei Nacht. Gauche: Vue de l'extérieur la nuit. | Right: Ground floor plan. Rechts: Grundriss. Droite: Plan du rez-de-chaussée.

The design for the Martini Hospital placed the new building next to one already halfway through its 40-year lifespan to be eventually replaced by a new building. Furthermore the function of the building can also become totally interchangeable in the design phase and when the building is in use. A nursing department can be converted to an outpatient clinic or offices, for example. Extensions can also be randomly attached to the façade to gain extra floor space allowing the accommodation of bigger departments. The only fixed elements are the service shafts, which will always remain at the center of the block.

Der Neubau für das Martini-Krankenhaus ist neben einem Gebäude geplant, dessen 40-jährige Nutzungsdauer bereits zur Hälfte abgelaufen ist und das später durch ein neues ersetzt werden soll. Andererseits ist die Gebäudefunktion während der Nutzung gänzlich austauschbar. So lässt sich beispielsweise eine Pflegeabteilung in eine Tagesklinik oder Büros umbauen. Zusätzliche Geschossflächen zur Unterbringung größerer Abteilungen lassen sich durch beliebige Anbauten an der Fassade realisieren. Die einzigen ortsfesten Elemente bilden die Versorgungsschächte, die immer im Gebäudekern verbleiben.

Un nouveau bâtiment a été construit près de l'ancien qui, après vingt ans de service, a déjà atteint la moitié de sa durée de vie et sera ultérieurement remplacé par un nouvel édifice. Les architectes ont conçu un bâtiment multifonctionnel en tenant compte de cette situation. C'est ainsi que la salle de soins actuelle pourra être transformée à terme en salle d'urgences ou en bureaux. De plus, des agrandissements sont toujours possibles si le besoin de place se faisait sentir. Les seuls éléments fixes de l'ensemble sont les couloirs logistiques intégrés au cœur du bâtiment.

Hallway toward patient rooms. Flur zu den Patientenzimmern. *Couloir menant aux chambres des patients.*

From left to right, from above to below:
Glazed façade, workspace, detail interior.
Right: Multi-story interior.

Von links nach rechts, von oben nach unten:
Verglaste Fassade, Arbeitsplatz, Einrichtungsdetail.
Rechts: Vielgeschossiger Innenraum.

De gauche à droite, de haut en bas:
Façade en verre, espace de travail, détail de l'intérieur.
Droite: Vue sur les étages.

CANNON DESIGN

www.cannondesign.com

Client: Baptist Medical Center, **Completion:** 2005, **Gross floor area:** 203,000 sq. ft., **Photos:** Robert Pettus Photography, St. Louis, MO (30 a.r.), Neil Rashba, Ponte Vedra, FL (28, 30 a.l., 30 b.l., 30 b.r., 31).

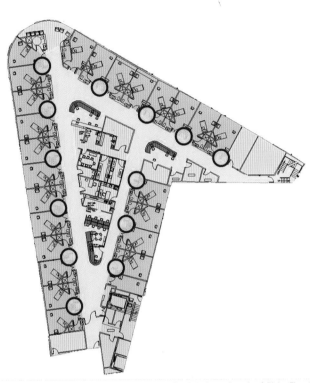

Left: Non-invasive Cardiology. Links: Nichtinvasive Kardiologie. Gauche: Cardiologie non invasive. | Right: Floor Plan. Rechts: Grundriss. Droite: Plan.

Signaling Baptist's leadership in cardiovascular care, the hospital establishes a landmark along Jacksonville's riverfront. Two stacked, independent vehicular drop-off loops provide centralized access to the 195,000 square-feet hospital, an expanded emergency room, and garage. Rising three stories, a freestanding helipad shelters drop-offs, creating a campus icon announcing the arrival experience. An extensive garden at the entry court extends into a cascading atrium connecting all four stories. The building responds to the flowing form of the nearby river, affording patient views of the skyline across the water.

Die Herzklinik übernimmt eine führende Rolle in der Behandlung von Herz-Kreislauf-Erkrankungen und bildet eine neue Landmarke an Jacksonvilles Flussufer. Zwei unabhängige Anfahrtsringe fungieren als zentrale Erschließung für die 18.116 m² große Herzklinik, die Notfallaufnahme und das Parkhaus. Der freistehende, über drei Ebenen aufsteigende Hubschrauberlandeplatz überdacht die Zufahrten. Ein ausgedehnter Garten am Eingangshof erstreckt sich bis zu einem kaskadenförmigen Atrium, das alle vier Geschosse miteinander verbindet. Da das Gebäude den geschwungenen Verlauf des nahegelegenen Flusses erwidert, können die Patienten auf die städtische Skyline am anderen Ufer blicken.

Ce bâtiment qui domine la rivière traversant Jacksonville illustre l'importance de l'église baptiste dans la région en ce qui concerne le traitement des maladies cardiovasculaires. Deux rampes en spirale indépendantes permettent aux véhicules d'accéder à cet hôpital de près de 6000 mètres carrés doté d'une salle d'urgence renforcée et d'un parking souterrain. La tour de trois étages qui supporte la plate-forme d'hélicoptère domine le campus et manifeste la modernité de l'ensemble. Au vaste jardin de la cour d'entrée succède une verrière qui interconnecte les quatre niveaux du bâtiment. La façade suit le cours de la rivière et les patients bénéficient d'une vue imprenable sur la ville.

From left to right, from above to below:
Entrance hall, terrace, helipad at night,
entry court with helipad.
Right: Patient room.

Von links nach rechts, von oben nach unten:
Eingangshalle, Terrasse, Hubschrauberlandeplatz
bei Nacht, Eingangshof mit Hubschrauberlandeplatz.
Rechts: Patientenzimmer.

De gauche à droite, de haut en bas:
Hall d'entrée, terrasse, plate-forme d'hélicoptère
de nuit, entrée avec plate-forme pour hélicoptère.
Droite: chambre des patients.

JESÚS IRISARRI CASTRO

Client: Consellería of Sanidade - Xunta of Galicia, **Completion:** 2006, **Gross floor area:** 2,400 m², **Photos:** Courtesy of Health Center.

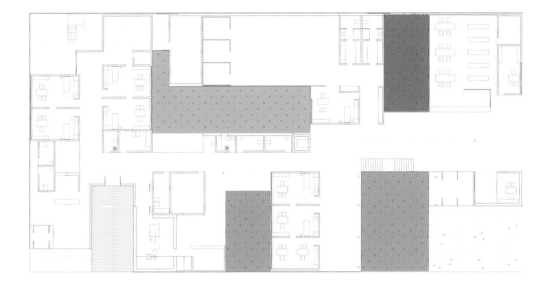

Left: Exterior view. Links: Außenansicht. Gauche: Vue de l'extérieur. | Right: Ground floor plan. Rechts: Erdgeschossplan. Droite: Plan du rez-de-chaussée.

The building is organized in two levels, the first one reflects the topographical richness; the second one echoes its degree of permeability or integration into the environment. The construction of the building has also followed the two-volume pattern. The volumes, although sharing the structural solution, differ in their outer shell, which gives them personal character. The volume including the surgery offices has a multilayer façade, whereas the waiting area is enclosed with double glazing. The outer layer of wood, opaque in the surgery area, gradually becomes lattice and finally disappears.

Der Bau ist in zwei Ebenen organisiert. Die erste spiegelt die topografische Vielfalt wider; die zweite greift den Grad seiner Durchlässigkeit oder Einbindung in das Umfeld auf. Auch die bauliche Anlage folgt dem Muster mit zwei Volumen. Obwohl die Gebäude konstruktiv gleich gelöst sind, unterscheiden sie sich in ihrer Außenhülle und erhalten so eine eigene, persönliche Note. Der Baukörper mit den Behandlungszimmern hat eine mehrschichtige Fassade, den Wartebereich hingegen umschließt eine Doppelverglasung. Die äußere Holzschicht ist im Behandlungsbereich undurchsichtig, geht allmählich in eine Gitterstruktur über, bis sie schließlich ganz verschwindet.

Ce bâtiment s'organise sur deux niveaux, le premier reflétant la topographie des lieux, le second le degré d'intégration dans l'environnement. Ses deux volumes ont une structure commune mais deux enveloppes distinctes qui les différentient. Celui qui abrite les cabinets de chirurgie est pourvu d'une façade multicouche, tandis que le volume des salles d'attente présente une façade en double vitrage. Le revêtement en bois, opaque du côté des cabinets de chirurgie, s'étiole progressivement pour former un treillis avant de disparaître totalement.

Interior view. Innenansicht. Vue de l'intérieur.

From left to right, from above to below:
View toward first floor with glazed waiting room,
exterior detail, glazed façade.
Right: View toward entrance.

Von links nach rechts, von oben nach unten:
Blick auf die erste Etage mit verglastem Wartezimmer,
Außendetail, verglaste Fassade.
Rechts: Blick auf den Eingang.

De gauche à droite, de haut en bas:
Vue sur le 1er étage avec salle d'attente vitrée,
détail extérieur, façade vitrée.
Droite: Vue sur l'entrée.

PETER AND PAULA FASSEAS CANCER CLINIC AT UNIVERSITY MEDICAL CENTER,
TUSCON, AZ, USA

CO ARCHITECTS

www.coarchitects.com
Client: University Medical Center, University of Arizona, Completion: 2007, Gross floor area: 82,000 sq. ft.,
Photos: Robert Canfield.

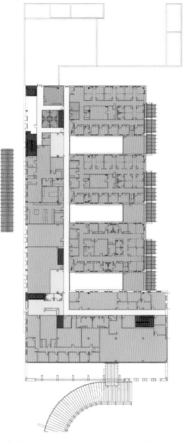

Left: Exterior view. Links: Außenansicht. Gauche: Vue extérieure. | Right: Floor plan. Rechts: Grundriss. Droite: Plan.

The architecture and nature are closely integrated through use of elements such as abundant daylight, trellised terraces, and vistas to beautiful mountain ranges beyond. All elements of the building's design are intended to relate to the natural landscape. A sense of beauty and calm is provided by a healing garden that is an integral part of the design. Arizona sandstone, plaster, and metal panels are used on the exterior. Trellises and covered entries provide shade from the sun. Interior finishes include natural materials or those made from natural products, such as stone flooring and wood paneling.

Architektur und Natur gehen durch reichlich Tageslicht, Terrassen mit Gitterwerk und Ausblicke auf die schöne Bergkette eine enge Verbindung ein. Alle Gestaltungselemente sollen sich auf die natürliche Landschaft beziehen. Ein Garten mit Heilpflanzen vermittelt einen Eindruck von Schönheit und Ruhe. An den Außenwänden finden sich Arizona-Sandstein, Putz und Metalltafeln. Pergolen und überdachte Eingänge schützen vor der Sonne. Die Innenausstattung besteht aus natürlichen Materialien oder solchen, die aus Naturprodukten hergestellt wurden, wie Steinböden und Holzvertäfelungen.

Cet hôpital intègre la nature environnante grâce à des terrasses agrémentées de treillis et à de grands espaces vitrés qui assurent un bon éclairage naturel et offrent des vues magnifiques sur les montagnes voisines. De fait, tous les éléments architecturaux visent ici à établir des liens avec la nature. C'est le cas notamment du jardin, qui contribue au processus de guérison par le calme et la beauté qui s'en dégagent. Les façades se composent de grès de l'Arizona, de panneaux métalliques et de surfaces enduites de plâtre. Des treillis protègent du soleil, notamment au niveau des entrées. Les aménagements intérieurs utilisent des matériaux naturels, en particulier le bois qu'on trouve sur le plancher et les murs.

Planted patio for recreation. Bepflanzter Innenhof zur Erholung. Cour intérieure arborée et espace de détente.

From left to right, from above to below:
View toward entrance, rear view,
space between volume.
Right: Roofed entrance.

Von links nach rechts, von oben nach unten:
Blick auf den Eingang, Rückansicht,
Raum zwischen dem Gebäude.
Rechts: Überdachter Eingang.

De gauche à droite, de haut en bas:
Vue sur l'entrée, arrière du bâtiment,
espace entre deux bâtiments.
Droite: Entrée couverte.

KAISER PERMANENTE PANORAMA CITY MEDICAL CENTER,
PANORAMA CITY, CA, USA

CO ARCHITECTS

www.coarchitects.com

Client: Kaiser Permanente Panorama City Medical Center, **Completion:** 2007, **Gross floor area:** 400,000 sq. ft., **Photos:** Robert Canfield.

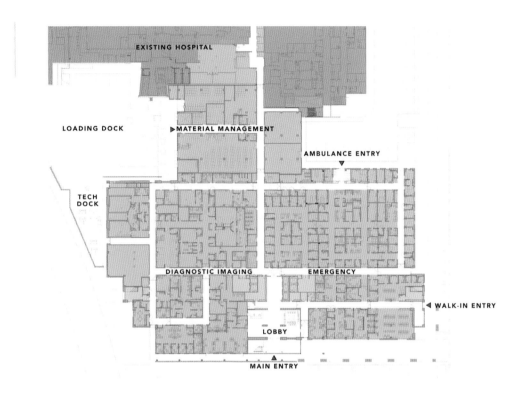

EXISTING HOSPITAL

LOADING DOCK

▶MATERIAL MANAGEMENT

AMBULANCE ENTRY
▽

TECH
DOCK

DIAGNOSTIC IMAGING

EMERGENCY

◀ WALK-IN ENTRY

LOBBY

▲
MAIN ENTRY

Left: Entrance view. Links: Eingangsbereich. Gauche: Vue sur l'entrée. | Right: Ground floor plan. Rechts: Erdgeschossplan. Droite: Plan du rez-de-chaussée.

The building is organized in a "bundled" vertical design that responds to the urban context of a constrained site. Support and diagnostic & treatment functions are located on the large, lower three floor plates, which are topped with three smaller floors of nursing unit functions. All floors are organized around an east-west oriented "core" of support functions. The clustering of core functions within the building also allows for large, open, flexible 'loft' space on the diagnostic & treatment floors for ever-changing functions such as operating rooms and imaging rooms.

Der „gebündelte" vertikale Entwurf des Gebäudes reagiert auf den städtischen Kontext eines beengten Grundstücks. Die großen, unteren drei Ebenen beherbergen Versorgungseinrichtungen sowie Diagnostik und Behandlung. Darüber sind drei kleinere Geschosse mit Pflegebereichen angeordnet. Alle Etagen sind um einen ostwestlich ausgerichteten „Kern" mit Versorgungsfunktionen organisiert. Die Bündelung zentraler Funktionen im Gebäude ermöglicht großzügige, offene und flexible „Loft"-Bereiche auf den Diagnostik- und Behandlungsgeschossen für sich stets verändernde Funktionen wie Operationssäle und Bildbetrachtungsräume.

Ce bâtiment s'organise selon un agencement vertical qui correspond au contexte urbain et aux dimensions réduites du terrain. Les salles de consultation et de soins ainsi que les services auxiliaires occupent les trois étages inférieurs, surmontés par trois autres étages en retrait abritant les chambres des patients. À l'intérieur du bâtiment, toutes les fonctions s'orientent le long d'un axe central qui va d'est en ouest. Les fonctions de base telles l'imagerie médicale et les salles d'opération sont regroupées dans de vastes espaces ouverts et flexibles qui ressemblent à des lofts.

Entrance hall. Eingangshalle. Hall d'entrée.

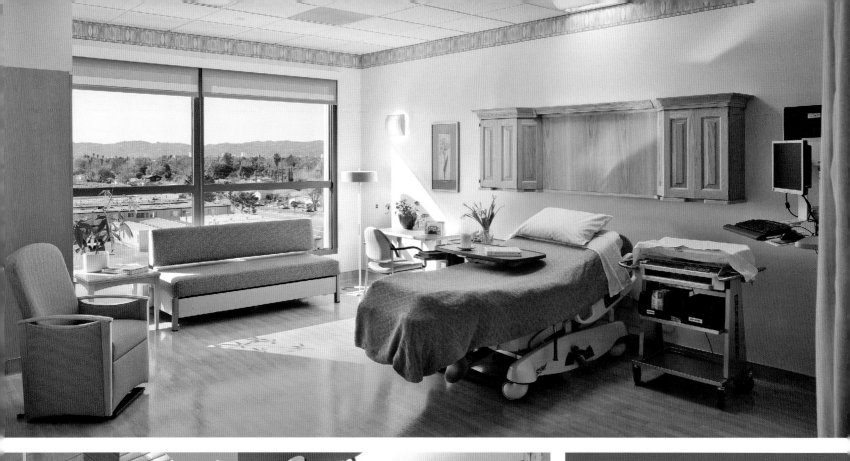

From left to right, from above to below:
Patient room, waiting room, detail entrance.
Right: Entrance view.

Von links nach rechts, von oben nach unten:
Patientenzimmer, Warteraum, Eingangsdetail.
Rechts: Eingangsbereich.

De gauche à droite, de haut en bas:
Chambre des patients, salle d'attente, détail de l'entrée.
Droite: Vue sur l'entrée.

PALOMAR MEDICAL CENTER WEST,
ESCONDIDO, CA , USA

CO ARCHITECTS

www.coarchitects.com

Client: Palomar Pomerado Health, **Completion:** 2011, **Gross floor area:** 736,000 sq. ft., **Renderings:** Courtesy of CO Architects.

CLEAN PROCEDURE

INTERVENTIONAL RADIOLOGY

PRE/POST OP

SURGERY

PATHOLOGY

PRE ADMIT

EXTERIOR COURTYARD

EXTERIOR COURTYARD

RESOURCE CENTER

CHAPEL

INPATIENT REHAB

PHARMACY

Left: Detail façade. Links: Fassadendetail. Gauche: Détail de la façade. | Right: Second floor plan. Rechts: Grundriss zweite Etage. Droite: Plan du 2e étage.

Using open floor plans with minimal vertical obstructions, the PMCW design can be adjusted to future interior and service needs. Extensive use of windows, interior courtyards, and rooftop gardens add nature to the hospital. A green rooftop garden filters rainwater before it enters municipal sewers, thus helping to clean storm run-off, while insulating the PMCW. The facility's many green features include an efficient lighting system, and recaptured waste heat. It is a pilot project using the Green Guide for Healthcare (GGHC), an architectural rating system based on the LEED model.

Da der PMCW-Entwurf offene Grundrisse mit minimalen vertikalen Behinderungen vorsieht, lässt er sich an den zukünftigen räumlichen und technischen Bedarf anpassen. Zahlreiche Fenster, Innenhöfe und Dachgärten holen die Natur ins Krankenhaus. Ein begrünter Dachgarten filtert das Regenwasser, bevor es der städtischen Kanalisation zugeführt wird. Zu den vielen umweltfreundlichen Elementen der Einrichtung gehören auch eine effiziente Belichtung und eine Abwärmerückgewinnung. Das Pilotprojekt nutzt den Green Guide for Healthcare (GGHC), ein architektonisches, auf dem LEED-Modell beruhendes Bewertungssystem.

Un plan avec un minimum de structures porteuses verticales garantit la possibilité de réaménager l'intérieur afin de satisfaire à de nouveaux besoins. De grandes baies vitrées ouvrent le bâtiment sur le paysage, tandis qu'un toit et des cours intérieures végétalisés introduisent l'élément naturel dans l'hôpital. Les plantes du toit filtrent par ailleurs l'eau de pluie et contribuent à l'isolation thermique du bâtiment. Parmi les nombreux équipements écologiques du complexe, citons notamment le système d'éclairage à efficacité accrue et l'installation de récupération de la chaleur. Ces équipements répondent à la norme GGHC (Green Guide for Healthcare), basée sur la norme architecturale LEED.

Exterior view by night. Außenansicht bei Nacht. Vue extérieure de nuit.

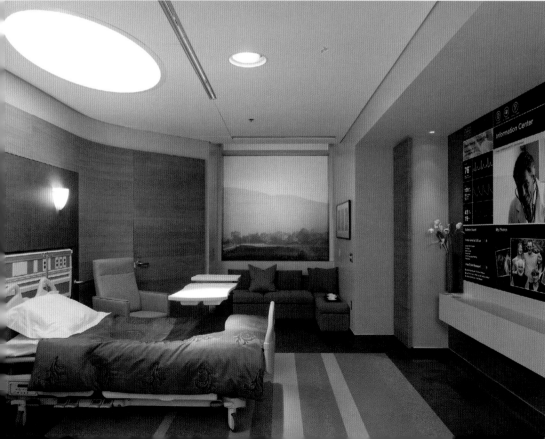

From left to right, from above to below:
Entrance hall, patient room, interior.
Right: Glazed façade.

Von links nach rechts, von oben nach unten:
Eingangshalle, Patientenzimmer, Inneneinrichtung.
Rechts: Verglaste Fassade.

De gauche à droite, de haut en bas:
Hall d'entrée, chambre des patients, intérieur.
Droite: Façade vitrée.

GREIFSWALD UNIVERSITY CLINICAL CENTER,
GREIFSWALD, GERMANY

DALL & LINDHARDTSEN A/S
ARCHITECTS

www.dall-lindhardtsen.de

Client: State of Mecklenburg-Western Pomerania, represented by Betrieb für Bau- und Liegenschaften Mecklenburg-Western Pomerania, Division Greifswald, **Completion:** 2003, **Gross floor area:** 812,380 sq. ft., **Photos:** Tobias Wille Photography.

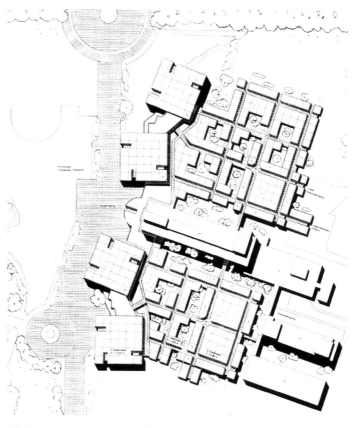

Left: Emergency entrance. Links: Notaufnahme. Gauche: Entrée des urgences. | Right: Site plan. Rechts: Lageplan. Droite: Plan du site.

The inner traffic network of this hospital can be expanded to accommodate potential future develop- ments. The various departments and clinic buildings constitute a modern hospital complex with different heights, green inner courtyards and glass corridors. The design focuses on the clear layout of the various networked areas and on the convenience of patients in terms of room fixtures and fittings and the pleas- ant design of examination and treatment rooms and staff working areas. Lateral skylight ribbons above the corridors and transparent façade sections pro- vide the buildings with natural light.

Die Abteilungen und Kliniken fügen sich aus Baukörpern mit unterschiedlichen Gebäudehöhen, begrünten Innenhöfen und verglasten Verbindungs- gängen zu einem modernen, kleinteilig gegliederten Krankenhauskomplex zusammen. Das innere Verkehrsnetz verknüpft die einzelnen Bereiche optimal und ist für Erweiterungen offen. Neben der übersichtlichen Organisation wurde großer Wert auf die angenehme und komfortable Gestaltung der Patientenzimmer, Behandlungsräume und Arbeits- bereiche gelegt. Seitliche Oberlichtbänder über den Fluren und transparente Fassadenfelder sorgen für eine natürliche Belichtung.

Le réseau de circulation intérieur de cet hôpital a été conçu de manière à pour pouvoir se développer en même temps que le bâtiment lui-même. Plusieurs immeubles de taille différente forment un complexe aux éléments reliés par des couloirs vitrés et des cours intérieures « vertes ». Les architectes ont mis l'accent sur un style clair et agréable, tant en ce qui concerne les chambres que les espaces médica- lisés, avec pour résultat un confort accru pour les patients. Des portions de façade transparentes et des bandes de fenêtres zénithales dans les couloirs assurent un bon éclairage naturel de l'intérieur.

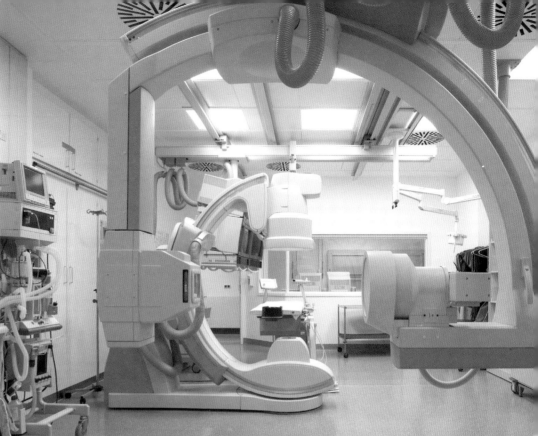

From left to right, from above to below:
Hallway, examination room, entrance hall.
Right: Exterior view.

Von links nach rechts, von oben nach unten:
Flur, Behandlungszimmer, Eingangshalle.
Rechts: Außenansicht.

De gauche à droite, de haut en bas:
Couloir, salle d'examens, hall d'entrée.
Droite: Vue extérieure.

GRAZ-WEST STATE HOSPITAL,
GRAZ, AUSTRIA

DOMENIG EISENKÖCK GRUBER

www.domenig.at, www.eisenkoeck.com, www.architekt-gruber.at
Client: Steiermärkische Krankenanstaltengesellschaft m.b.H. (KAGes), Completion: 2002, Gross floor area:
335,712 sq. ft., Photos: Paul Ott.

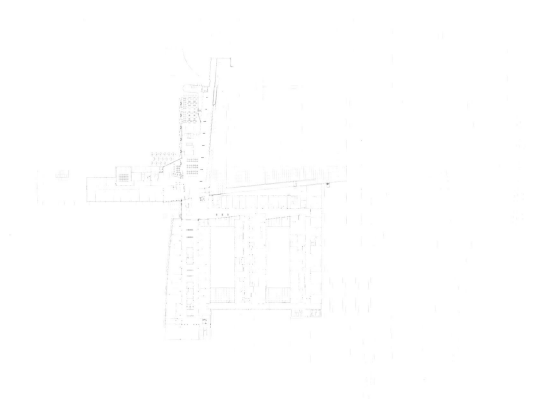

Left: Exterior view. Links: Außenansicht. Gauche: Vue extérieure. | Right: Ground floor plan. Rechts: Erdgeschossplan. Droite: Plan du rez-de-chaussée.

The new lightweight cross-shaped building with a re-inforced concrete skeleton and partition walls, has a long main cross section with low cube-like structures placed in front of it at a right angle. Towards the rear, the two-floor "special class wing" completes the form of the cross. The entrance leads to a two-floor hall with a gallery, cafeteria, kiosk and waiting areas. The conference and patients' rooms were designed with hotel levels of comfort and the open outdoor spaces structured as patients' gardens. Natural materials and glass were used inside.

Der kreuzförmige Neubau, ein Stahlbetonskelett-Bau mit Zwischenwänden in Leichtbauweise, hat einen langen Hauptriegel, dem im rechten Winkel ein Flügel mit niedrigen, kubischen Baukörpern vorgelagert ist. Der zweigeschossige Sonderklassetrakt ist orthogo-nal zum Haupttrakt ausgerichtet. Der Haupteingang führt in eine Halle mit Galerie, Café, Kiosk und War-tezonen. Aufenthaltsbereiche und Patientenzimmer sind in Hotel-Komfort gestaltet und das Freiland wur-de als Patientengarten angelegt. Im Inneren wurden natürliche Materialien und Glas verwendet.

Cet immeuble en croix se compose d'une structure porteuse en béton armé et d'une enveloppe légère. La barre principale et la barre secondaire, plus base, se coupent à angle droit. L'aile « classe spéciale » de deux étages qui se trouve à l'arrière du bâtiment vient compléter l'ensemble. Le hall d'entrée sur deux niveaux donne accès à un café, un kiosque à journaux et une galerie marchande ainsi qu'aux salles d'attente. Les salles de réunions et les chambres n'ont rien à envier aux grands hôtels en matière de confort. Les abords de l'hôpital sont aménagés en jardins. La décoration intérieure est à base de verre et de matériaux naturels.

From left to right, from above to below:
Detail façade, atrium, façade.
Right: Glazed entrance hall.

Von links nach rechts, von oben nach unten:
Fassadendetail, Atrium, Fassade.
Rechts: Verglaste Eingangshalle.

De gauche à droite, de haut en bas:
Détail de la façade, atrium, façade.
Droite: Hall d'entrée vitrée.

HOSPITAL REGIONAL DE ALTA ESPECIALIDAD,
MÉRIDA, MEXICO

DUARTE AZNAR ARQUITECTOS, S.C.P

www.duarteaznar.com
Client: Yucatán State Government, **Completion:** 2007, **Gross floor area:** 45,000 m², **Photos:** Roberto Cárdenas Cabello.

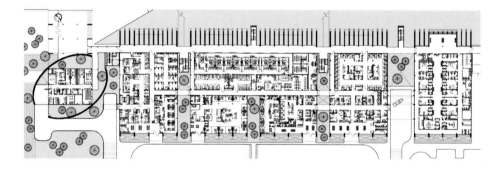

Left: Exterior view. Links: Außenansicht. Gauche: Vue extérieure. | Right: Ground floor plan. Rechts: Grundriss Erdgeschoss. Droite: Plan du rez-de-chaussée.

Based on the investigations of Roger S. Ulrich and his proposals on comprehensive design, this project incorporated aspects that are of privilege to the patients of the mechanical operation. Constant interaction with exteriors was allowed, and since the inhabitants are more familiarized with the exterior, the project resorted to profuse native vegetation, besides conserving the existing trees, and to promote shade, while improve airflow naturally. Privacy is obtained with porches restricting the view of interior spaces, while suppressing corridor and doctors offices to allow lines of vision to the outside.

Ausgehend von Roger S. Ulrichs Untersuchungen und seinem ganzheitlichen Ansatz beinhaltet dieses Projekt Aspekte, die sich auf den Aufenthalt im Krankenhaus günstig auswirken. So wird den Patienten ein ständiger Zugang zum Außenbereich ermöglicht, der üppig mit einheimischen Pflanzen gestaltet ist; vorhandene Bäume wurden erhalten und die Luftströmung auf natürliche Weise verbessert. Für Privatsphäre sorgen Veranden, die den Blick in die Innenräume einschränken, während Flur und Arztzimmer Blickachsen nach draußen gewähren.

Cet immeuble conçu d'après le principe de « design intégral » développé par Roger S. Ulrich intègre divers aspects qui sont le privilège de patients devant subir une opération chirurgicale. L'intérieur reste constamment en contact avec l'extérieur et puisque les patients vivent habituellement en plein air, l'édifice a été construit en préservant les arbres qui se trouvaient à l'origine sur le terrain. Ceux-ci offrent désormais de l'ombre et contribuent naturellement à la circulation d'air. L'agencement intérieur figure des porches qui garantissent l'intimité des patients tout en offrant des perspectives sur l'extérieur.

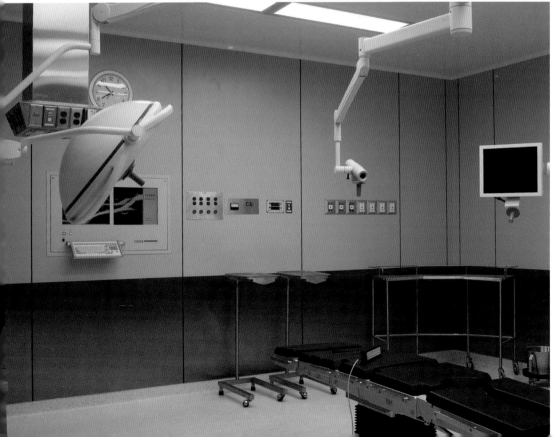

From left to right, from above to below:
Waiting hall, operating theater, exterior stair.
Right: Passage between two volumes.

Von links nach rechts, von oben nach unten:
Wartehalle, Operationssaal, Außentreppe.
Rechts: Übergang zwischen zwei Gebäuden.

De gauche à droite, de haut en bas:
Hall d'attente, salle d'opérations, escalier extérieur.
Droite: Passage entre deux bâtiments.

DAIMIEL'S HEALTH CARE CENTER – OUTPATIENT SPECIALTY CENTER,
DAIMIEL, SPAIN

ESTUDIO ENTRESITIO

www.entresitio.com

Client: Castilla-La Mancha Regional Health Service, **Completion:** 2007, **Gross floor area:** 5,300 m²,
Photos: Raul Belichón.

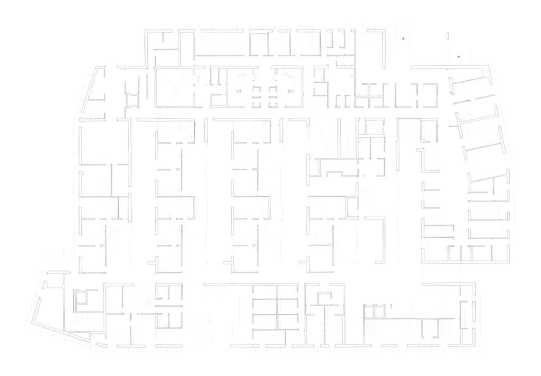

Left: Metallic skin of louvers. Links: Verkleidung mit metallischen Luftschlitzen. Gauche: Revêtement fait de panneaux fins de métal. | **Right:** Ground floor plan. Rechts: Grundriss Erdgeschoss. Droite: Plan du rez-de-chaussée.

On the outside, the project solves the image of a public building fitted in a housing neighbourhood, being covered with a metallic skin of louvers made out of micro perforated galvanized plates that helps loosing the scale of every single window. Inside, the building is open to five patios cladded with a galvanized ondulated sheet, with the consultations on one side and circulations and waiting areas on the other side, maximising optimal conditions of natural lighting and ventilation through the glazed enclosures. The interior is made of white materials, mosaic tiles, compact laminate panels and glass.

Von außen wirkt das Projekt wie ein öffentliches Gebäude in einer Wohnbebauung. Dieser Eindruck entsteht durch seine jalousieartige Metallverblendung aus mikroperforierten verzinkten Platten, welche nicht die Größe der einzelnen Fenster zu erkennen geben. Innen öffnet sich der Bau zu fünf Innenhöfen, die mit verzinktem Wellblech verkleidet sind. Da die Beratungszimmer auf der einen Seite liegen und die Verkehrswege und Wartezonen auf der anderen, werden die Bedingungen für eine natürliche Belichtung und Belüftung durch gläserne Umfassungen optimiert. Für die Innengestaltung wurden weiße Materialien, Mosaikfliesen, Laminatplatten und Glas verwendet.

Ce nouvel hôpital de trois cents lits répartis sur trois niveaux a une taille humaine. Dominant un vallon, il crée un contraste entre la rusticité du paysage et le raffinement technologique de son architecture. De hautes fenêtres structurent la façade en verre sérigraphié. La juxtaposition horizontale des pôles d'activité offre une grande visibilité, facilite la circulation à l'intérieur du bâtiment et permettra des agrandissements ultérieurs. La couleur joue un rôle important dans les cours plantées d'arbres : les teintes des différents matériaux y structurent l'espace et soulignent l'apport essentiel de l'art à cet hôpital.

From left to right, from above to below:
Detail façade, entrance view,
metallic skin, inner courtyard.
Right: Front view.

Von links nach rechts, von oben nach unten:
Fassadendetail, Eingangsansicht,
metallische Verkleidung, Innenhof.
Rechts: Vorderansicht.

De gauche à droite, de haut en bas:
Détail de la façade, vue sur l'entrée,
revêtement en métal, cour intérieure.
Droite: Vue frontale.

THUNDER BAY REGIONAL HEALTH SCIENCES CENTER,
THUNDER BAY, ON, CANADA

FARROW PARTNERSHIP
ARCHITECTS INC.

www.farrowpartnership.com
Client: Thunder Bay Regional Health Sciences Center, Completion: 2004, Gross floor area: 650,000 sq. ft.,
Photos: Peter Sellar; KLICK Photography.

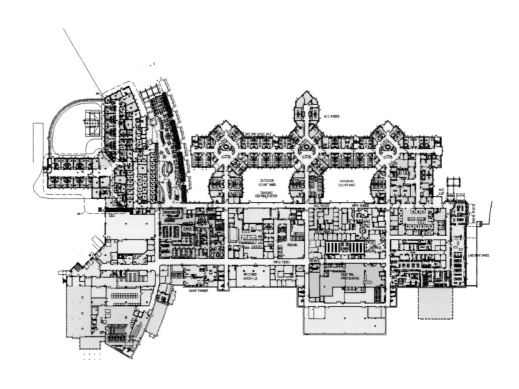

Left: Entrance area. Links: Eingangsbereich. Gauche: Vue sur l'entrée. | Right: First floor plan. Rechts: Grundriss erste Etage. Droite: Plan du 1er étage.

This Thunder Bay Center project is a 650,000 square-feet design, occupied by 375 beds, and is an acute care regional hospital that opened in February 2004. The hospital includes all acute care services, forensic mental health, a helicopter pad, and base hospital facilities to serve all of North Western Ontario. Furthermore, the complex includes the 68,000 square-feet North Western Ontario Regional Cancer Center. Embracing humanism, the multiple-height interior spaces flooded with natural light, create dynamic, innovative, and functional places for healing.

Das Projekt Thunder Bay Center beinhaltet eine Geschossfläche von 60.387 m². Das regionale Akutkrankenhaus mit 375 Betten eröffnete im Februar 2004. Vorhanden sind das gesamte Spektrum der Akutversorgung, eine Abteilung für Forensische Psychiatrie, ein Hubschrauberlandeplatz sowie Einrichtungen der Regelversorgung für den Nordwesten Ontarios. Außerdem gehört zu dem Komplex das 6.317 m² große Krebszentrum North Western Ontario Regional Cancer Center. Auf der Grundlage humanistischer Prinzipien schaffen mehrgeschossige lichterfüllte Räume ein dynamisches, innovatives und funktionelles Umfeld für die Genesung.

Ce complexe hospitalier régional de 375 lits et d'une superficie totale d'environ 200 000 mètres carrés a ouvert en février 2004. Il dispose d'équipements pour tous les types de soins intensifs et psychiatriques, ainsi que d'une plate-forme d'hélicoptère lui permettant d'accueillir des patients venus de tout le nord-ouest de l'Ontario. Un centre de cancérologie couvrant plus de 20 000 mètres carrés en fait également partie. L'intérieur, de conception humaniste, inclut des espaces de différentes hauteurs baignés de lumière naturelle. Cet agencement dynamique, novateur et fonctionnel a un effet bénéfique sur le processus de guérison.

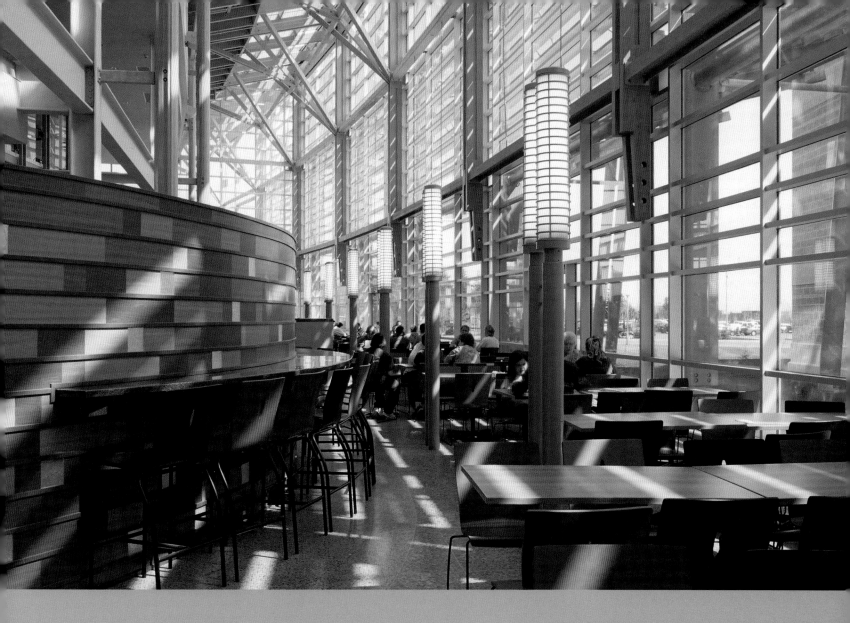

From left to right, from above to below:
Staircase, aerial view, detail exterior, detail construction.
Right: Cafeteria.

Von links nach rechts, von oben nach unten:
Treppe, Luftbild, Außendetail, Konstruktionsdetail.
Rechts: Cafeteria.

De gauche à droite, de haut en bas:
Escalier, vue aérienne, détail extérieur, détail de construction.
Droite: Cafétéria.

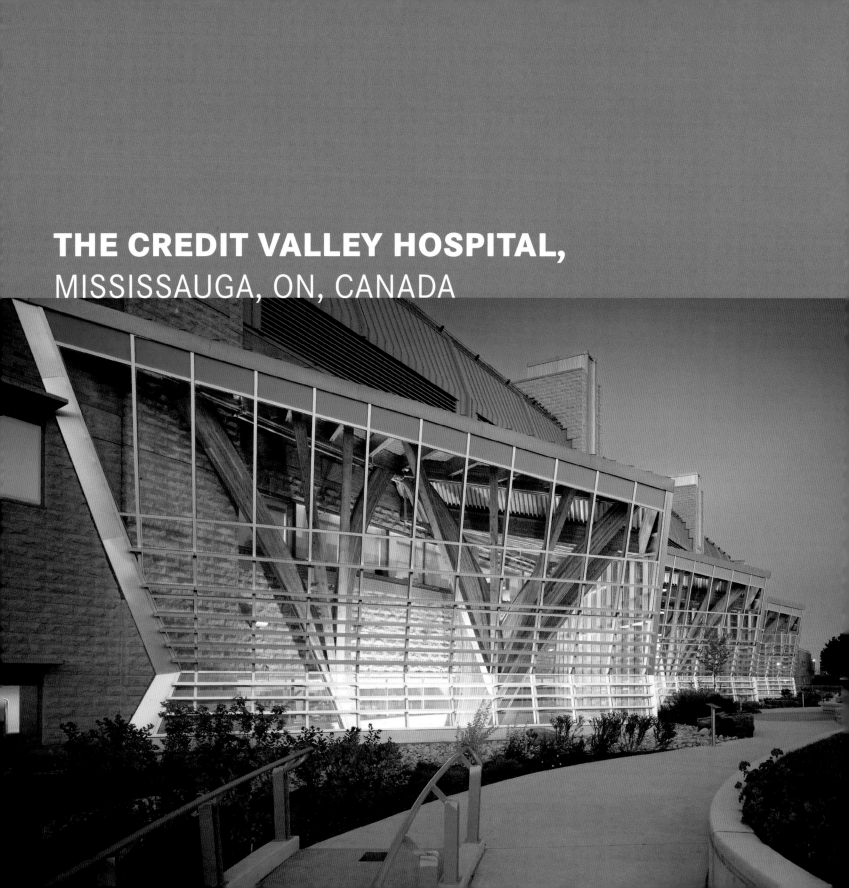

THE CREDIT VALLEY HOSPITAL,
MISSISSAUGA, ON, CANADA

FARROW PARTNERSHIP ARCHITECTS INC.

www.farrowpartnership.com
Client: The Credit Valley Hospital, **Completion:** 2005, **Gross floor area:** 320,000 sq. ft., **Photos:** Shai Gil; Peter Sellar, KLIK Photography.

Left: **Exterior view.** Links: Außenansicht. Gauche: Vue extérieure. | **Right: Site plan.** Rechts: Lageplan. Droite: Plan du site.

Farrow Partnership Architects Inc. designed The Credit Valley Hospital's 320,000 sq. ft. Cancer Care and Ambulatory Care facility, which includes features such as Complex Continuing Care, Rehabilitation, Maternal Child Care, Laboratory Services, and Emergency Room renovations. These renovations and additions are only phase one for a larger three-phase, $349 million dollar project, designed to serve the future health care needs for the people of Mississauga. The dramatic spaces and warm materials of the new facility promote humanistic healing practices among patients and staff.

Farrow Partnership Architects Inc. konzipierten für das Credit Valley Hospital eine Einrichtung für Krebsbehandlung und ambulante Versorgung auf 29.729 m². Zum Auftrag gehörten der Umbau der Bereiche für Komplexe Fortgesetzte Versorgung, Rehabilitation, Mutter-Kind-Behandlung, Laboruntersuchungen und Notfallaufnahme. Diese Umbauten und Erweiterungen sind die erste von insgesamt drei Phasen eines Projekts mit einem Volumen von 349 Millionen Dollar. Sie sollen die zukünftige Krankenversorgung in Mississauga sicherstellen. Die aufsehenerregenden Räume und behaglichen Materialien der neuen Einrichtung unterstützen die Anwendung humanistischer Heilmethoden.

Ce centre de cancérologie d'environ 100 000 mètres carrés a été conçu par Farrow Partnership Architects Inc. On y trouve une gamme complète de services, allant du traitement continu à la rééducation en passant par les soins à la mère et l'enfant, les laboratoires d'analyses et les salles d'urgence. Les travaux de rénovation et d'extension constituent la première phase d'un projet de 349 millions de dollars destiné à couvrir les besoins sanitaires de la population de Mississauga. Des espaces vastes et des matériaux chaleureux vont dans le même sens que les méthodes de traitement humanistes appréciées aussi bien des patients que du personnel soignant.

Street side view. Straßenansicht. Vue latérale depuis la rue.

From left to right, from above to below:
Entrance hall, curved benches,
wood and glass cladding, detail construction.
Right: Floor painting.

Von links nach rechts, von oben nach unten:
Eingangshalle, bogenförmige Bänke,
Holz- und Glasverkleidung, Konstruktionsdetail.
Rechts: Bodenbemalung.

De gauche à droite, de haut en bas:
Hall d'entrée, bancs de forme ovale,
ossatures en bois et en verre, détail de construction.
Droite: Peinture au sol.

KNITTELFELD STATE HOSPITAL,
KNITTELFELD, AUSTRIA

FASCH & FUCHS
WITH LUKAS SCHUMACHER

www.faschundfuchs.com
Client: Steiermärkische Krankenanstaltengesellschaft m.b.H. (KAGes), **Completion:** 2005, **Gross floor area:** 98,626 sq. ft., **Photos:** Paul Ott.

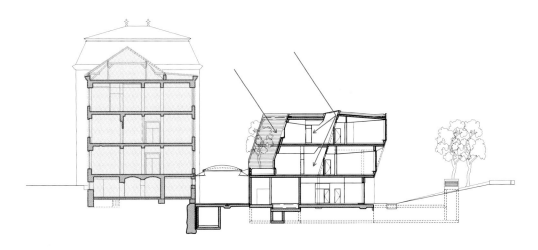

Left: Glazed façade. Links: Verglaste Fassade. Gauche: Façade vitrée. | Right: Section. Rechts: Schnitt. Droite: Coupe.

The three-floor extension will be located immediately north of the existing building. Short distances guarantee the best connection between the outpatient departments and the sickrooms. The sickrooms on the first and second floors open onto the tree-planted landscape via glass sections spanning the whole room width. In the basement, the space between the two parallel wings is used as a farmyard with a translucent membrane roof. Openings in the extension structure the outside area and the wards' halls. Daylight enters the halls through the tree-planted courtyards, creating an inviting atmosphere with regular views into the surrounding.

Der dreigeschossige Anbau wird unmittelbar nördlich des Bestandes angeordnet. Kurze Wege garantieren die bestmögliche Verbindung zwischen Ambulanzen und Krankenzimmern. Die Krankenzimmer in den Obergeschossen öffnen sich über raumbreite Verglasungen in die Landschaft. Der Raum zwischen den parallel angeordneten Trakten ist mit einer transluzenten Membram überdacht und wird als Wirtschaftshof genutzt. Einschnitte im Anbau strukturieren zugleich den Außenraum und die Gänge der Stationen. Über die Höfe fällt Tageslicht in die Gänge und erzeugt ein einladendes Raumgefüge mit regelmäßigen Ausblicken in die Umgebung.

La nouvelle annexe sur trois niveaux se dresse juste à côté du bâtiment ancien de manière à assurer une bonne liaison entre les espaces réservés aux malades hospitalisés et ceux fréquentés par les patients bénéficiant de soins externes. Les chambres situées au premier et au second étage donnent sur un espace planté d'arbres par l'intermédiaire d'une façade en verre. L'espace souterrain qui s'étend entre les deux ailes parallèles est couvert par un toit transparent et abrite des animaux. Diverses ouvertures structurent les façades de l'annexe. Un éclairage naturel crée une atmosphère agréable à l'intérieur de l'hôpital.

Exterior staircase. Außentreppe. Escalier extérieur.

From left to right, from above to below:
Roofed access road, hallway, meeting area.
Right: Exterior view.

Von links nach rechts, von oben nach unten:
Überdachte Zufahrt, Flur, Aufenthaltsraum.
Rechts: Außenansicht.

De gauche à droite, de haut en bas:
Tunnel couvert, couloir, espace d'accueil.
Droite: Vue extérieure.

87

BÖBLINGEN DISTRICT HOSPITAL,
BÖBLINGEN, GERMANY

FREUDENFELD + KRAUSEN + WILL ARCHITECTS

www.fkw-a.de
Client: Kreiskliniken Böblingen gGmbH, Completion: 2006, Gross floor area: 177,002 sq. ft., Photos: Freudenfeld + Krausen + Will Architects.

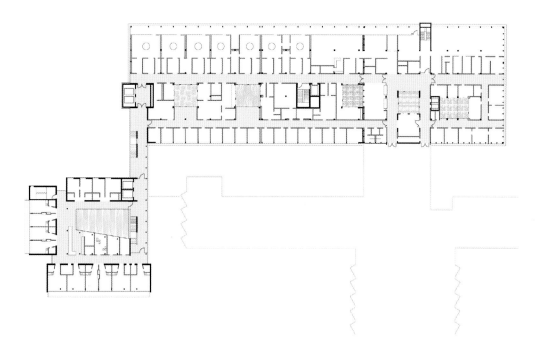

Left: Exterior view. Links: Außenansicht. Gauche: Vue extérieure. | Right: Third floor plan. Rechts: Grundriss dritte Etage. Droite: Plan du 3e étage.

The plan included rebuilding and gradually extending the central functional building and the construction of a new children's hospital. Subsequently, two existing buildings from different periods were converted into one structure. Its metal glass exterior clearly sets the building apart from the massive brickwork façades of the other buildings on the hospital grounds. Green courtyards let daylight into the center of the compact structure. Waiting and recreational areas, connected by linear corridors, run tangent to the courtyards and offer various views and sources of daylight.

Die längerfristige Zielplanung sah den Bau der neuen Kinderklinik vor. Zudem wurden zwei Bestandsbaukörper verschiedener Entstehungszeit schrittweise zu einem zentralen Funktionsbau umgestaltet. Durch seine Metall-Glas-Haut unterscheidet er sich auffällig von den massiven Klinkerfassaden der übrigen Gebäude auf dem Klinikgrundstück. Eine Folge begrünter Höfe lenkt Tageslicht ins Zentrum des kompakten Baukörpers. An sie lagern sich Warte- und Aufenthaltszonen an, verbunden durch ein lineares Flursystem, das die Höfe tangential begleitet. So entsteht eine Sequenz wechselnder Blick- und Lichtbezüge.

Ce complexe est le résultat d'un plan d'ensemble prévoyant la rénovation et l'agrandissement progressif d'un ancien complexe hospitalier, ainsi que la construction d'un nouvel hôpital pour enfants. Deux bâtiments construits à des périodes différentes ont été réunis par une structure en verre et métal qui se distingue nettement des bâtiments en briques plus anciens. Des cours « vertes » permettent à la lumière du jour de pénétrer jusqu'au centre de cette structure compacte. Des zones de repos et des salles d'attente reliées par des couloirs linéaires offrent des vues sur les alentours et contribuent également à l'éclairage naturel de l'intérieur.

From left to right, from above to below:
Staircase, workspace,
exterior patient rooms, wooden sun screen.
Right: Atrium.

Von links nach rechts, von oben nach unten:
Treppenhaus, Arbeitsplatz, Außenansicht der
Patientenzimmer, hölzerne Sonnenblenden.
Rechts: Atrium.

De gauche à droite, de haut en bas:
Escalier, espace de travail, vue extérieure sur
les chambre des patients, pare-soleil en bois.
Droite: Atrium.

PEDIATRIC CLINIC "PRINCESS MARGARET",
DARMSTADT, GERMANY

ANGELA FRITSCH ARCHITEKTEN

www.af-architekten.de

Client: Foundation Alice-Hospital by the Red Cross Darmstadt, **Completion:** 2006, **Gross floor area:** 4,950 m², **Photos:** Prof. Dieter Leistner, Würzburg.

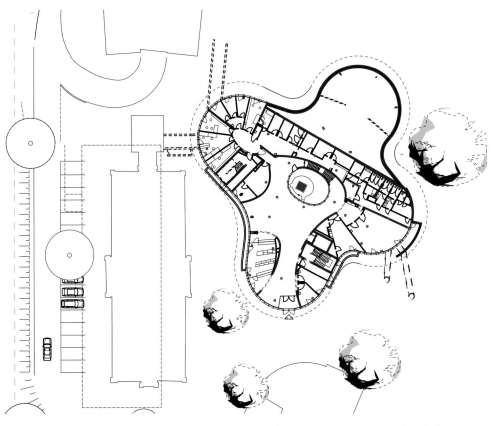

Left: Foyer steles. Links: Stelen im Foyer. Gauche: Installations dans le foyer. | Right: Ground floor plan. Rechts: Grundriss Erdgeschoss. Droite: Plan du rez-de-chaussée.

The 80-bed children's hospital was constructed in the park of the Alice hospital near Mathildenhöhe in Darmstadt. Its petal-shaped design is particularly suited to this setting. The patients' rooms are located on the two upper floors, while the treatment and auxiliary rooms are on the ground floor, which simultaneously serves as an entrance and reception area. The hospital stay is not intended to shut the children off from the outside world in a sterile hospital environment, but to stimulate them with new impressions, thus contributing to their healing.

Die Kinderklinik mit 80 Betten wurde im Park des Alicehospitals an der Mathildenhöhe in Darmstadt errichtet. Durch die Blütenform fügt sie sich städtebaulich besonders gut in die Umgebung ein. Die Patientenzimmer befinden sich in den beiden Obergeschossen, die Behandlungs- und Nebenräume im Erdgeschoss, welches zugleich als Eingangs- und Empfangsbereich dient. Der Aufenthalt in der Klinik, soll die Kinder in der klinisch sterilen Umgebung eines Krankenhauses nicht von der Welt außerhalb abschotten, sondern sie mit neuen Wahrnehmungen animieren und so zur Gesundung beitragen.

Cette clinique pour enfants de quatre-vingt lits est une dépendance de l'hôpital de Darmstadt. Sa forme en trèfle à quatre feuilles s'adapte parfaitement à l'implantation dans un parc. Les chambres se trouvent aux étages supérieurs, l'accueil, les salles de soins et les locaux techniques au rez-de-chaussée. Les architectes ont évité l'atmosphère stérile qu'on trouve habituellement dans les hôpitaux, et cherché à stimuler la perception des jeunes patients afin de favoriser le processus de guérison.

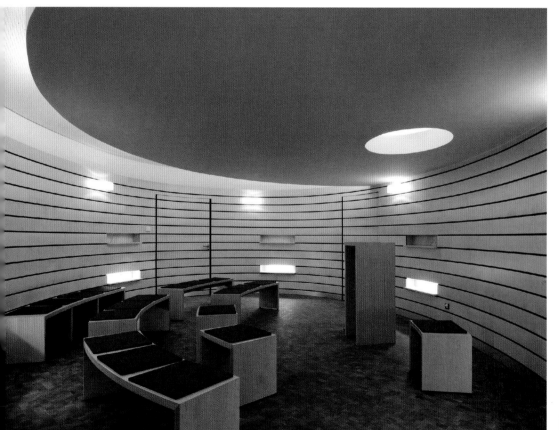

From left to right, from above to below:
Floor painting, painted hallway, bereavement room, hallway.
Right: Foyer with steles and seating islands.

Von links nach rechts, von oben nach unten:
Bodenbemalung, bemalter Flur, Trauerraum, Flur.
Rechts: Eingangsbereich mit Stelen und Sitzinseln.

De gauche à droite, de haut en bas:
Peinture au sol, couloir décoré, salle de recueillement, couloir.
Droite: Espace à l'entrée avec stèles et îlots pour s'asseoir.

PAN PRAXISKLINIK AM NEUMARKT,
COLOGNE, GERMANY

GATERMANN + SCHOSSIG

www.gatermann-schossig.de
Client: Neumarkt Immobiliengesellschaft & Co. KG, Completion: 1999, Gross floor area: 6,500 m²,
Photos: Jens Willebrand, Cologne.

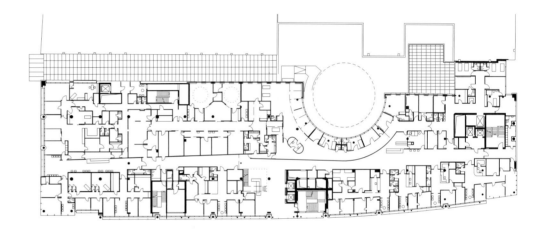

Left: Hallway with information desk. Links: Flur mit Informationstheke. Gauche: Couloir et bureau d'informations. | Right: Third floor plan.
Rechts: Grundriss dritte Etage. Droite: Plan du 3e étage.

A two-floor hospital center was built on the basis of the steel concrete structure of a former warehouse. It features a comprehensive medical infrastructure with 17 specialized departments as well as a surgical center with outpatient and inpatient clinics. To facilitate orientation within the clinic, the individual style of the furnishings was highlighted by the use of various materials. Light and friendly colors combine with the warm wood tones of the fixtures to create a pleasant atmosphere.

In der Stahlbetonstruktur eines ehemaligen Warenhauses entstand auf zwei Etagen ein Klinikzentrum, das über eine umfassende medizinische Infrastruktur mit 17 verschiedenen Fachbereichen sowie ein operatives Zentrum mit einer Tagesklinik und einem stationären Bereich verfügt. Um die Orientierung innerhalb der Klinik zu erleichtern, wurde das individuelle Erscheinungsbild der Einrichtungen durch die Verwendung verschiedener Materialien hervorgehoben. Helle und freundliche Farben schaffen in Verbindung mit den warmen Holztönen der Einbauten eine angenehme Atmosphäre.

Cette clinique sur deux étages a été aménagée dans un ancien grand magasin en béton armé. Elle offre une infrastructure médicale complète, avec dix-sept services différents, un bloc opératoire, un espace pour les patients hospitalisés et un autre pour les patients externes. L'aménagement intérieur utilise divers matériaux de manière à différentier les espaces et à faciliter l'orientation. Des couleurs claires et sympathiques, associées aux tons chauds du bois des meubles, créent une atmosphère agréable à l'intérieur de la clinique.

Klinik-Aufnahme

From left to right, from above to below:
Wood cladding, luminous panels, entrance hall,
information desk and staircase.
Right: Information desk.

Von links nach rechts, von oben nach unten:
Wandvertäfelung, leuchtende Paneele,
Eingangshalle, Infromationstheke und Treppenhaus.
Rechts: Informationstresen.

De gauche à droite, de haut en bas:
Revêtements en bois, panneaux lumineux,
hall d'entrée, bureau d'informations et escalier.
Droite: Bureau d'informations.

ÄRZTEHAUS RODENKIRCHEN KÖLN,
COLOGNE, GERMANY

GATERMANN + SCHOSSIG

www.gatermann-schossig.de
Client: Forum Immobilien GmbH Köln, **Completion:** 2002, **Gross floor area:** 9,686 m², **Photos:** Jens Willebrand, Cologne.

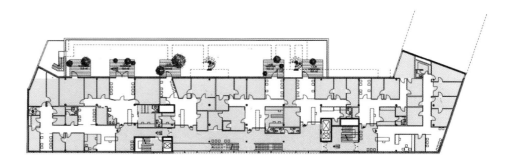

Left: Glazed façade. Links: Verglaste Fassade. Gauche: Façade vitrée. | Right: First floor plan. Rechts: Grundriss erste Etage. Droite: Plan du 1er étage.

The building lives from the outer appearance of the restrained shimmering body and the extensive glazing of the three-story entrance hall. This light-flooded open space connects the shops on the ground floor to the practices above, thus creating a weather-proof, communicative area. A further feature of the building is the stair tower, which connects all floors and has a warm wood-coloring, generating a contrast to steel and glass. The material wood re-appears in the flooring of the hall and the practices above. Towards the hall, each practice receives its own primary color, revealed towards the open main road on a backlit glass wall.

Der zurückhaltende weiß-silberne Baukörper wirkt nach außen durch die großflächige Verglasung der dreigeschossigen Eingangshalle lebendig. Die lichtdurchflutete Halle verbindet die Läden im Erd-geschoss mit den darüberliegenden Arztpraxen und schafft einen kommunikativen Ort. Der Treppenturm prägt den Komplex zusätzlich durch seine warme Holzverkleidung, die Stahl und Glas kontrastiert. Holz findet sich in den Bodenbelägen der Halle wieder und fließt in den Obergeschossen bis in die Praxen hinein. Jede Praxis erhält eine ihr eigene Grundfarbe, die in einer hinterleuchteten Glaswand zur Magistrale hin präsentiert wird.

Ce bâtiment se caractérise par son enveloppe miroitante et la surface vitrée sur trois étages du hall d'entrée, espace de communication baigné de lumière naturelle qui donne accès aux boutiques du rez-de-chaussée et aux cabinets médicaux des étages supérieurs. L'autre caractéristique de l'édifice est sa cage d'escalier où des tons de bois chaleu-reux contrastent avec l'aspect froid du métal et du verre. Le bois est également utilisé pour le parquet du hall d'entrée et des cabinets médicaux. Ceux-ci se distinguent par une couleur qui leur est particu-lière et qu'on aperçoit du côté de la rue grâce à une façade en verre rétro-éclairée.

Luminous wall panels. Leuchtende Wandpaneele. Panneaux lumineux au mur.

From left to right, from above to below:
Detail exterior, entrance view, staircase,
luminous wall panels.
Right: Hallway.

Von links nach rechts, von oben nach unten:
Außendetail, Eingangsansicht, Treppenhaus,
leuchtende Wandpaneele.
Rechts: Flur.

De gauche à droite, de haut en bas:
Détail extérieur, vue sur l'entrée, escalier,
panneaux lumineux au mur.
Droite: Couloir.

THEORETIKUM – RESEARCH CENTER OF THE UNIVERSITY HOSPITAL,
JENA, GERMANY

GERBER ARCHITECTS

www.gerberarchitekten.de
Client: Free State of Thuringia, **Completion:** 2003, **Gross floor area:** 33,571 sq. ft., **Photos:** Hans Jürgen Landes.

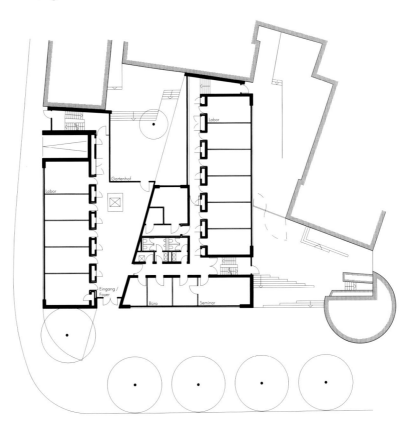

Left: Entry front. Links: Eingangsfassade. Gauche: Façade de l'entrée. | Right: Ground floor plan. Rechts: Grundriss Erdgeschoss. Droite: Plan du rez-de-chaussée.

The three-floor, U-shaped central research building is based on the old Baroque building as seen by its compact ground plan and the height of its ceilings, its façade structure and the color design. It surrounds a greened inner courtyard that is connected to the already existing buildings. The side of the building facing the road and the inner courtyard are glazed, creating a harmony between the old and the new building. Due to the fact that it is based on the historical building, the architectural elements seem reduced and serve the functionality of the building.

Das dreigeschossige Forschungsgebäude in U-Form orientiert sich mit seinem kompakten Grundriss, seiner Geschosshöhe, der Fassadengliederung und Farbgestaltung an der barocken Altbebauung. Die herausragende Stellung des Turmes der Anatomie bleibt somit erhalten. Gemeinsam mit den bestehenden, denkmalgeschützten Gebäuden umschließt der Neubau einen begrünten Innenhof. Alt- und Neubau harmonieren durch die Verglasung zur Straße und zum Hof hin. Wegen seiner historischen Orientierung erscheinen die architektonischen Elemente reduziert und an die Sachlichkeit des Gebäudezwecks ausgerichtet.

Le centre de recherche sur trois niveaux s'inspire des couleurs, de la façade, du plan compact et des hauteurs de plafond du bâtiment baroque qui le jouxte. L'immeuble moderne en forme de U entoure une cour « verte » fermée sur le quatrième côté par l'ancien édifice. Le verre de la façade côté rue et la verrière de la cour intérieure assure l'harmonie de l'ensemble. La proximité du bâtiment classé a contraint les architectes à privilégier des éléments architecturaux sobres et fonctionnels lors de la conception du nouvel édifice.

From left to right, from above to below:
Historical and new façade,
view to the garden courtyard, entrance hall.
Right: View from the garden courtyard to the entrance hall.

Von links nach rechts, von oben nach unten:
Historische und neue Fassade,
Blick auf den Garten, Eingangshalle.
Rechts: Blick vom Innenhof auf die Eingangshalle.

De gauche à droite, de haut en bas:
Ancienne et nouvelle façade, vue sur le jardin, hall d'entrée.
Droite: vue du jardin intérieur sur le hall d'entrée.

CARDIAC CENTER OF THE UNIVERSITY HOSPITAL ,
COLOGNE, GERMANY

GMP – VON GERKAN, MARG AND PARTNERS ARCHITECTS

www.gmp-architekten.de

Client: The University Hospital of Cologne, **Completion:** 2007, **Gross floor area:** 30,000 m², **Photos:** Jürgen Schmidt, Cologne.

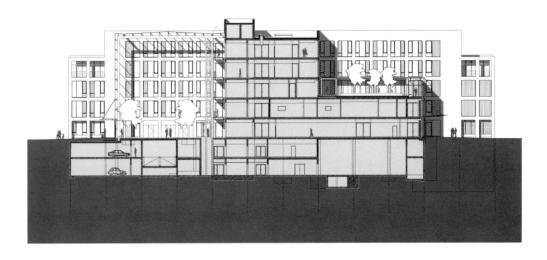

Left: 12-meter-high entrance. Links: 12-Meter hoher Eingang. Gauche: Entrée de 12 mètres de haut. | Right: Longitudinal section. Rechts: Längsschnitt. Droite: Coupe longitudinale.

Equipped with the latest medical equipment, the Cardiac Center welcomes patients and visitors with a glazed 12 meter-high entrance and a full height bright lobby. Deciduous trees with benches and warm materials such as cherry wood make the five-floor lobby attractive with an atmosphere resembling more a hotel than a clinic. The children's cardiology department on the second floor has a parents' room and playroom linked to a playground framed by green pergolas. The column beam façade of the new H-shaped building is clad in light shell limestone with reddish-tinted aluminum shades on the classical façade.

Das mit modernster Medizintechnik ausgestattete Herzzentrum empfängt die Patienten und Besucher mit einem verglasten 20 Meter hohen Eingangsportal und einer hellen haushohen Eingangshalle. Laubbäume, Sitzbänke und warme Materialien wie Kirschholz vermitteln in der fünfgeschossigen Eingangshalle eine Atmosphäre, die eher an ein Hotel als an ein Klinikgebäude erinnert. In der Kinderkardiologie in der zweiten Etage sind Eltern- und Spielzimmer mit einem von begrünten Pergolen gerahmten Spielhof im Freien verbunden. Die klassische Fassade des H-förmigen Baukörpers ist mit hellem Muschelkalk verkleidet und wird durch die Anordnung von rötlich schimmernden Alumium-Verschattern strukturiert.

L'accès à ce centre de cardiologie bénéficiant des derniers équipements médicaux se fait par un hall d'entrée vitré de douze mètres de haut. Des bancs, des arbres et des matériaux aux tons chauds comme le merisier lui confèrent une atmosphère qui évoque moins un hôpital qu'un hôtel de luxe. Le service de cardiologie pour enfants, situé au second étage, dispose d'une salle pour les parents et d'une salle de jeux reliée à une aire de jeux entourée de pergolas. Les façades de cet immeuble en forme de H sont de deux types : revêtement en panneaux calcaires légers pour la partie moderne et plaques d'aluminium teinté de rouge pour la partie classique.

Patio. Innenhof. Cour intérieure.

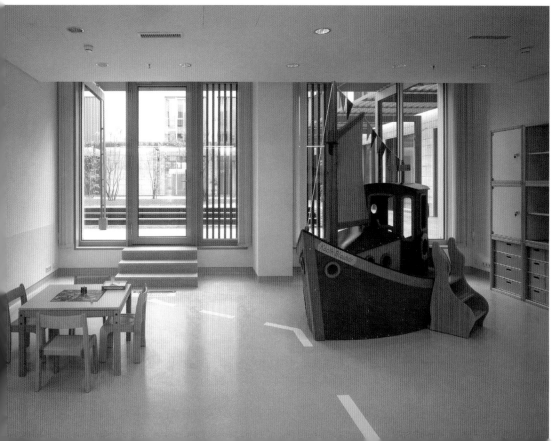
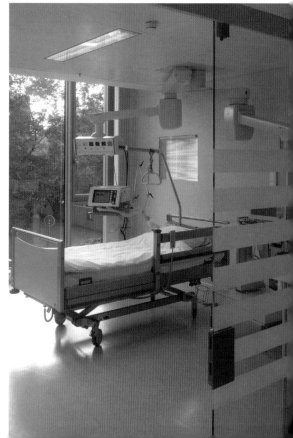

From left to right, from above to below:
Entrance hall, planted and muted colored vestibule,
children's unit, intensive care unit.
Right: Courtyard and roof terrace.

Von links nach rechts, von oben nach unten:
Eingangshalle, bepflanzter Vorhof in gedeckten Farben,
Kinderstation, Intensivstation.
Rechts: Innenhof und Dachterrasse.

De gauche à droite, de haut en bas:
Hall d'entrée, cour avant arborée et colorée,
secteur des enfants, salle de soins intensifs.
Droite: Cour intérieure et terrasse sur toit.

RAVELO MEDICAL CLINIC,
RAVELO, TENERIFE, SPAIN

GPY ARQUITECTOS

www.gpyarquitectos.com
Client: Canary Islands Government: Health and Consum, Completion: 2007, Gross floor area: 706 m², Photos: Efrain Pintos.

Left: Exterior view, driveway. Links: Außenansicht, Zufahrt. Gauche: Vue extérieure, accès. | Right: First floor plan. Rechts: Grundriss erste Etage. Droite: Plan du 1er étage.

The building has been designed with two levels and street-level pedestrian access. The main floor is occupied by the medical surgeries, while the lower floor houses multipurpose, administrative and staff areas. The project is characterized by a dialogue between the external, concrete frame, and an internal wooden layer that transforms the empty space of the frames into a series of rooms, separating the areas for specific private use from the public ones. To the north, the panoramic window embraces the distant countryside, incorporating it into the everyday life of the clinic.

Der Entwurf des Gebäudes umfasst zwei Ebenen und einen Fußgängerzugang auf Straßenniveau. Das Hauptgeschoss enthält die Chirurgie, die untere Ebene Multifunktions-, Verwaltungs- und Personalräume. Charakteristisch für das Projekt ist ein Dialog zwischen der äußeren Schicht, dem Beton-„Rahmen", und einer inneren Holzschicht, die den „gerahmten" freien Raum in eine Reihe von Zimmern umgestaltet. Dabei erfolgt eine Trennung zwischen den spezifischen Privatbereichen und den öffentlichen Zonen. Im Norden umrandet das Panoramafenster die Aussicht auf die weitläufige Landschaft und bezieht sie in den Alltag der Klinik ein.

Les piétons venant de la rue ont un accès direct à cet immeuble sur deux niveaux. Les locaux médicaux sont situés au niveau principal, tandis que les bureaux, les locaux du personnel et les espaces multifonctionnels se trouvent au rez-de-chaussée. L'ensemble se caractérise par un contraste entre le béton de l'extérieur et le bois des espaces intérieurs publics et privés. Les baies vitrées de la façade nord offrent des vues panoramiques sur la campagne environnante, qui se trouve ainsi intégrée au quotidien de la clinique.

Glazed façade. Verglaste Fassade. Façade vitrée.

From left to right, from above to below:
Driveway, access, waiting area, surgery.
Right: Reception.

Von links nach rechts, von oben nach unten:
Auffahrt, Eingang, Wartebereich, Sprechzimmer.
Rechts: Empfang.

De gauche à droite, de haut en bas:
Allée, accès au bâtiment, salle d'attente,
cabinet de consultation.
Droite: Réception.

MUNICIPAL CLINICAL CENTER BRANDENBURG / HAVEL,
BRANDENBURG / HAVEL, GERMANY

HEINLE, WISCHER UND PARTNER,
FREIE ARCHITEKTEN,
RESPONSIBLE PARTNERS: ROBERT
WISCHER, EDZARD SCHULTZ

www.heinlewischerpartner.de

Client: Städtisches Klinikum Brandenburg GmbH, **Completion:** 2003, **Gross floor area:** 14.457 m², **Photos:** Bernadette Grimmenstein.

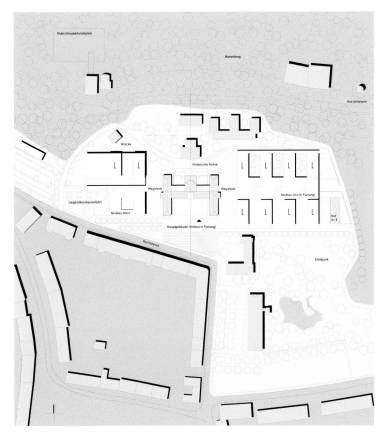

Left: New west building. Links: Neubau West. Gauche: Nouveau bâtiment ouest. | Right: Site plan. Rechts: Lageplan. Droite: Plan du site.

The design concept is a cross-shaped overlay of the old axis by a new glass corridor, which links the old H-shaped main building to the new buildings to the east and the west. Color, light and materials were key elements in the project. The ten operating theaters are located at the side of the building and therefore enjoy natural daylight. The colorful walls in the examination areas have a calming effect. The ceilings in the intensive care rooms have floral patterns, providing variety to patients lying in bed. The walls in the patient rooms are covered in wood, integrating all technical and medical equipment.

Leitgedanke ist die kreuzförmige Überlagerung der historischen Achse mit einer gläsernen Magistrale. Auf drei Ebenen verbindet diese das alte H-förmige Hauptgebäude mit den Neubauten in Ost und West. Von großer Bedeutung sind die Aspekte Farbe, Licht und Materialität. Die zehn an der Hausfassade liegenden OP-Säle beleuchtet Tageslicht. Die Farbgestaltung der Untersuchungsbereiche wirkt beruhigend, florale Muster an den Decken der Intensivstation bieten dem Blick der Patienten Abwechslung. In die Holzverkleidungen der Patientenzimmer sind sämtliche medizintechnischen Funktionen integriert.

La transformation d'un bâtiment ancien en forme de H a eu pour résultat un ensemble en forme de croix après l'ajout d'une unité en verre qui relie l'immeuble d'origine aux nouvelles ailes construites à l'est et à l'ouest. Les éléments clés du projet étaient la lumière, la couleur et les matériaux. Les dix salles d'opération situées dans une aile latérale bénéficient d'un bon éclairage naturel. Les couleurs qui animent les murs des salles de consultation ont un effet tranquillisant sur les patients. Les fleurs au plafond des salles de soins intensifs permettent aux malades alités de bénéficier d'une vue moins monotone qu'à l'accoutumée. Tous les équipements médicaux des chambres sont cachés derrière un revêtement de mur en bois.

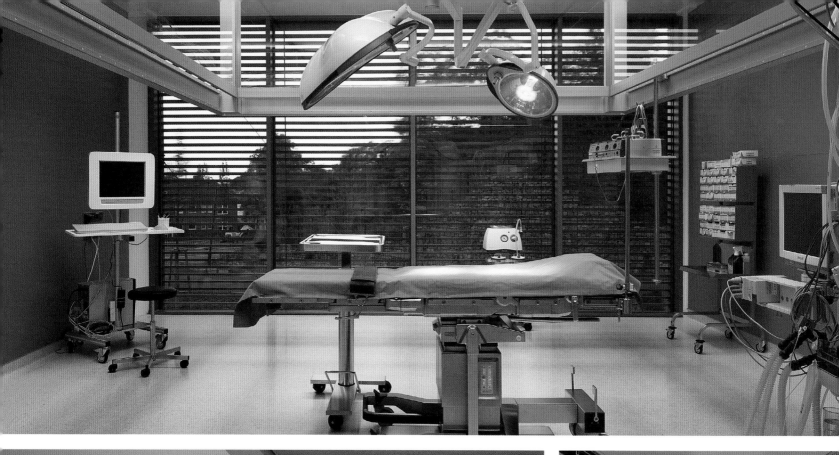

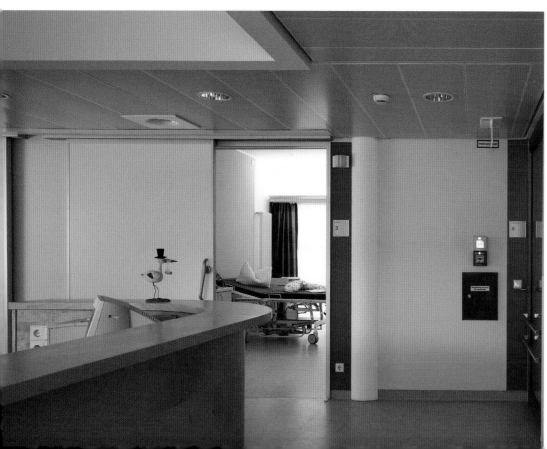

From left to right, from above to below:
Operating theater,
base delivery, glass main axis.
Right: Main axis.

Von links nach rechts, von oben nach unten:
Operationssaal, Stützpunkt Entbindung,
gläserne Magistrale.
Rechts: Magistrale.

De gauche à droite, de haut en bas:
Salle d'opérations, base du accouchent,
extension vitrée du bâtiment.
Droite: Escalier.

UNIVERSITY CLINICAL CENTER
CARL GUSTAV CARUS,
DRESDEN, GERMANY

HEINLE, WISCHER UND PARTNER,
FREIE ARCHITEKTEN,
RESPONSIBLE PARTNER
URSULA WILMS

www.heinlewischerpartner.de
Client: Free State of Saxony, Saxon State Ministry of Finance, represented by Public Enterprise Saxon property and Construction Management, **Completion:** 2003, **Gross floor area:** 30.037 m², **Photos:** Jörg Schöner, Bernadette Grimmenstein.

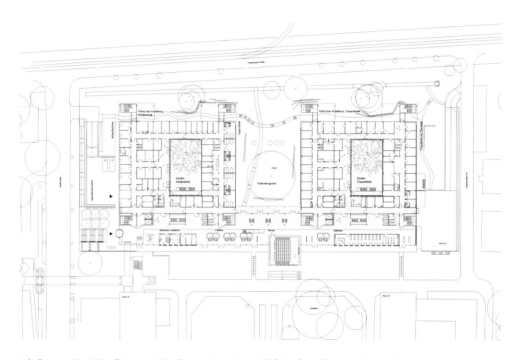

Left: Entrance view. Links: Eingangsansicht. Gauche: Vue sur l'entrée. | Right: Ground floor plan. Rechts: Grundriss Erdgeschoss. Droite: Plan du rez-de-chaussée.

The idea was to improve orientation within the building despite its complex services, with a special focus on daylight and transparency, views, and clear directions. The building has an easily identifiable color concept. The roofs are planted with greenery for environmental reasons and to make them more attractive when viewed from above. The flexible distribution of rooms enables different future use. The new entrance area next to the stretcher and emergency entrance leads to a planted garden hall. The adjacent outpatient wards, the lecture theater, seminar rooms, and school rooms can also be accessed from it.

Konzeptionelles Anliegen war es, trotz komplexer Nutzung leichte Orientierung im Gebäude zu ermöglichen. Dabei wurde besonderer Wert auf Tageslicht, Sichtbezüge und eine klare Wegeführung gelegt. Ein durchgängiges Farbkonzept kennzeichnet das Gebäude. Sämtliche Dächer sind aus ökologischen und ästhetischen Gründen extensiv begrünt. Die flexible Raumaufteilung gestattet spätere Umnutzungen. Der neue Eingangsbereich mit benachbartem Liegendkranken- und Notfalleingang führt zu einer vorgelagerten Gartenhalle. Von hier besteht direkter Zugang zu den Ambulanzen, zum Hörsaal, den Seminar- und Schulungsräumen.

Les architectes ont ici cherché à faciliter l'orientation à l'intérieur d'un bâtiment complexe, tout en mettant l'accent sur la transparence, l'éclairage naturel et la vue sur les alentours. Un concept de couleur facilement assimilable structure l'ensemble du bâtiment. Les toits sont plantés d'arbres pour des raisons tant esthétiques qu'environnementales. Les différents espaces ont une distribution flexible qui permet une grande variété d'affectations. Le hall d'entrée situé à proximité des urgences donne accès à une verrière aménagée en jardin, ainsi qu'aux salles de soins externes, à l'amphithéâtre et aux salles de cours.

Lobby in garden hall. Empfang Gartenhalle. Hall du jardin.

From left to right, from above to below:
Garden, gallery of garden hall,
nursing room, control station.
Right: Main hallway at nursing station.

Von links nach rechts, von oben nach unten:
Garten, Galerie der Gartenhalle,
Pflegezimmer, Leitstelle.
Rechts: Hauptflur Pflege.

De gauche à droite, de haut en bas:
Jardin, galerie de hall du jardin,
chambre des sous, salle de contrôle.
Droite: Couloir de l'étage des soins.

OSTALB CLINICAL CENTER, CLINIC HOTEL,
AALEN, GERMANY

HEINLE, WISCHER AND PARTNER, FREIE ARCHITEKTEN

www.heinlewischerpartner.de

Client: Ostalb Clinical Center, **Completion:** 2006, **Gross floor area:** 10,998 m², **Photos:** Hanno Chef, Stuttgart.

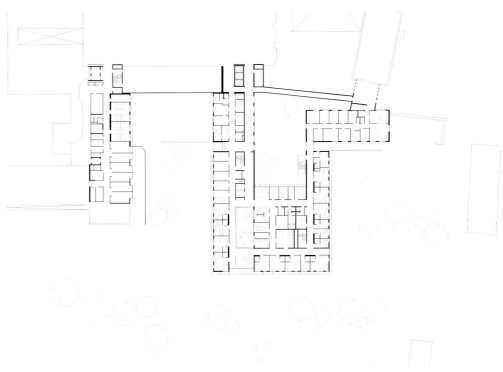

Left: Clinical center at hillside. Links: Klinikhotel am Hang. Gauche: Centre clinique à flanc de coteau. | Right: Ground floor plan. Rechts: Grundriss Erdgeschoss. Droite: Plan du rez-de-chaussée.

The hotel hospital is attached to the southern part of the existing structure. Sunlight enters each patient room throughout the day. Room-high glazing allows the patients to see the surrounding landscapes from their beds. In the shared bedrooms each patient is also near a window. Colored strips inserted into the façade change the atmosphere of the rooms in line with the changing sunlight. Optimized individual comfort, lovely views, attractive lounge areas, a clear structure, and a friendly atmosphere, all combine to stimulate the well-being and thus the convalescence of the patients.

Das Klinikhotel fügt sich südlich an das bestehende Ensemble an. Alle Patientenzimmer haben im Tagesverlauf Sonnenlicht. Raumhohe Verglasungen ermöglichen dem im Bett liegenden Patienten den Blick in die umgebende Landschaft. Auch in den Mehrbettzimmern verfügt jeder Patient über einen eigenen Fensterplatz. Durch in die Glasfassade eingesetzte bunte Streifen verändert sich je nach Sonneneinstrahlung die Atmosphäre des Raumes. Die Optimierung der individuellen Behaglichkeit, schöne Ausblicke ins Freie, ein attraktives Angebot an Aufenthaltsbereichen, Übersichtlichkeit und eine freundliche Atmosphäre fördern in hohem Maße das Wohlbefinden und damit die Genesung der Patienten.

Cet hôtel-clinique complète un ensemble préexistant. Toutes les chambres bénéficient d'éclairage naturel. Des pans de murs entièrement vitrés offrent à tous les patients alités des vues sur le paysage environnant, et cela même dans les chambres à plusieurs lits. L'atmosphère change continuellement dans les chambres du fait des plaques de couleur translucides insérées dans la façade. Afin de favoriser le processus de guérison, les architectes ont cherché à augmenter le bien-être des patients en leur offrant des vues panoramiques et en créant une ambiance agréable tant dans les chambres que dans les espaces communs.

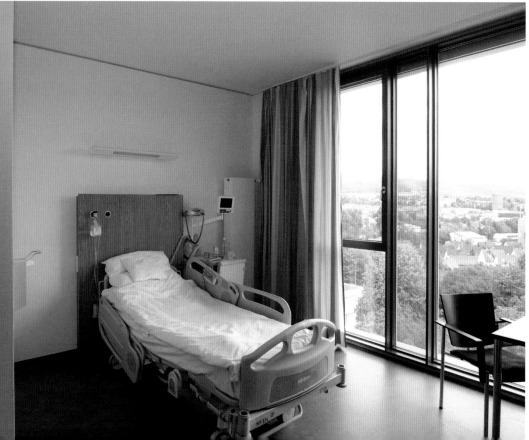

From left to right, from above to below:
Children's play area, meeting area for patients and visitors,
single patient room, control center and inner courtyard.
Right: Lobby.

Von links nach rechts, von oben nach unten:
Spielbereich für Kinder, Aufenthaltsbereich für
Patienten und Besucher, Einzelzimmer, Leitstelle und Innenhof.
Rechts: Empfang.

De gauche à droite, de haut en bas:
Espace de jeu pour enfants, salle d'attente pour patients et
visiteurs, chambre individuelle, vue sur le centre
de contrôle et la cour intérieure.
Droite: hall.

REHAB BASLE,
BASLE, SWITZERLAND

HERZOG & DE MEURON

Client: REHAB Basel AG, **Completion:** 2002, **Gross floor area:** 246,296 sq. ft., **Photos:** Margherita Spiluttini.

Left: Exterior view. Links: Außenansicht. Gauche: Vue extérieure. | Right: Floor plan. Rechts: Grundriss. Droite: Plan.

The building is a horizontal, two-story handicap-accessible complex. The treatment and examination facilities are on the ground floor and the patients' rooms are on the first floor. Courtyards provide daylight. While the gymnasiums, workshops and generously glazed patients' rooms face the landscape, other areas, such as the bathhouse, face the building's interior. Various types of wood, frequently in combination with textiles, are the prevailing materials of the façades, interior rooms and ceilings. Ornamental and kitchen gardens are planned south of the complex.

Der Bau ist eine horizontale, zweigeschossige Anlage mit leichter Zugänglichkeit für Rollstuhlfahrer. Im Erdgeschoss befinden sich die Therapie- und Untersuchungseinrichtungen, im ersten Obergeschoss die Bettenzimmer. Höfe führen Tageslicht ins Innere. Während Turnhalle, Werkstätten und Patientenzimmer mit großzügiger Verglasung auf die Landschaft weisen, sind andere Bereiche wie das Badehaus nach innen gerichtet. Vorherrschendes Material der Fassaden, Innenräume und Decken sind verschiedene Holzarten, die oft mit Textilien verbunden sind. Im Süden der Anlage sollen Zier- und Nutzgärten entstehen.

Cet immeuble sur deux niveaux est facilement accessible aux handicapés. Le rez-de-chaussée abrite les salles de consultation et de soins, tandis que les chambres aux vastes baies vitrées sont situées au premier étage. Plusieurs cours assurent une bonne diffusion de la lumière naturelle à l'intérieur du bâtiment. Les ateliers et les chambres offrent des vues sur le paysage environnant. Les espaces fonctionnels — notamment ceux consacrés à l'hydrothérapie — donnent sur l'intérieur du bâtiment. Diverses essences de bois, souvent combinées à des matériaux textiles, donnent une touche particulière aux aménagements intérieurs. Un jardin d'agrément doublé d'un potager s'étend au sud du complexe.

From above to below, from left to right:
Terrace, view outside, balcony.
Right: Inner courtyard.

Von oben nach unten, von links nach rechts:
Terrasse, Blick nach draußen, Balkon.
Rechts: Innenhof.

De gauche à droite, de haut en bas:
Terrasse, vue sur l'extérieur, balcon.
Droite: Cour intérieure.

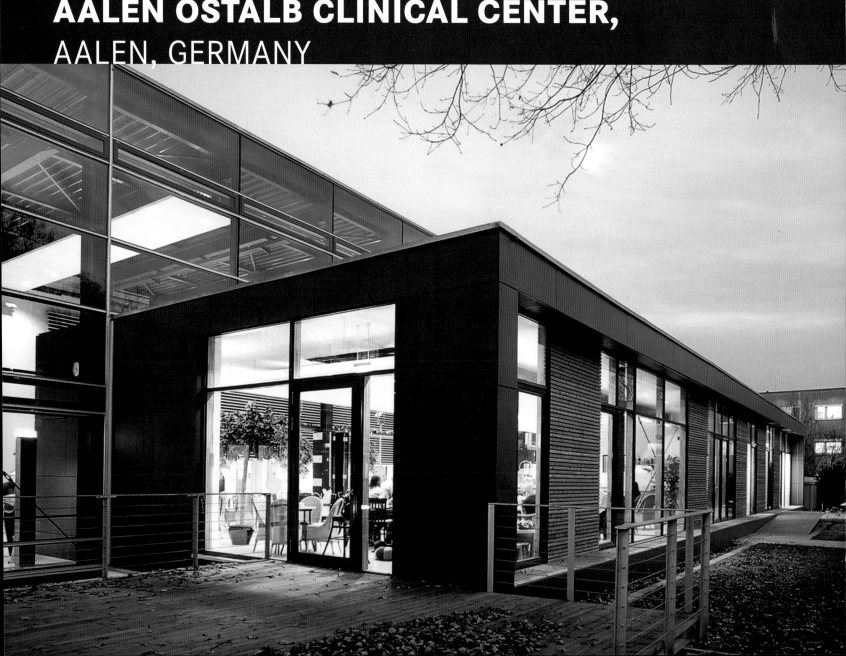

IAP ISIN ARCHITEKTEN GENERALPLANER

www.isin.de
Client: District of Ostalb, **Completion:** 2004, **Gross floor area:** 96,668 sq. ft., **Photos:** Fotostudio Spectrum, Ankenbrand.

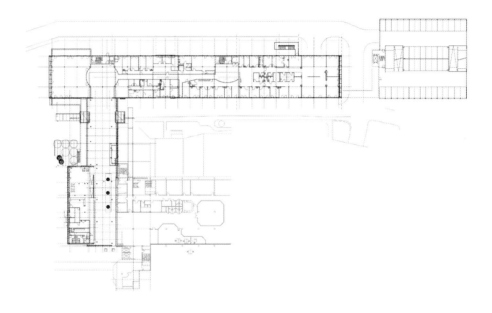

Left: Exterior view cafeteria. Links: Außenansicht Cafeteria. Gauche: Vue extérieure sur la cafétéria. | Right: Floor plan. Rechts: Grundriss. Droite: Plan.

The entrance is a reception area with a communication zone and a cafeteria, whose colors, materials and openness dispel the typical hospital atmosphere. The medical service center has a flexible structural design. It is connected to the entrance forum, i.e. the entire clinic, by five cubes linked by four inner courtyards. The cubes with their quadratic ground plans can be extended for additional use and are illuminated by the inner courtyards. The service center includes doctors' surgeries, speech and occupational therapists, consultancies, and day hospitals. The building is also equipped for ecological energy use.

Empfang und Cafeteria brechen in Farbe, Materialien und Übersichtlichkeit die typische Krankenhausatmosphäre auf. Für das ans Eingangsforum und die gesamte Klinik angeschlossene Medizinische Dienstleistungszentrum war eine flexible Baukonstruktion notwendig: Sie besteht aus fünf Kuben mit quadratischen Grundrissen. Diese sind über vier Innenhöfe verbunden und belichtet. Das Zentrum ist für zusätzliche Nutzungen erweiterbar. Zu den bisherigen Nutzern zählen Arztpraxen, Logopäden und Ergotherapeuten, Beratungen und Tageskliniken. Das Gebäude wurde nach ökologischen Gesichtspunkten gestaltet.

Le hall d'entrée est un espace de communication doté d'une cafétéria. Ses couleurs, ses matériaux et son aspect ouvert annoncent d'emblée l'atmosphère caractéristique de cette clinique. Il s'agit d'un complexe flexible, composé de cinq cubes reliés entre eux par quatre cours intérieures. Les plans carrés des cubes permettent des agrandissements ultérieurs, tandis que les cours assurent un bon éclairage naturel. La clinique se compose de différents services (chirurgie, thérapie verbale et occupationnelle) et d'espaces réservés aux soins externes. Le complexe intègre par ailleurs un concept énergétique respectueux de l'environnement.

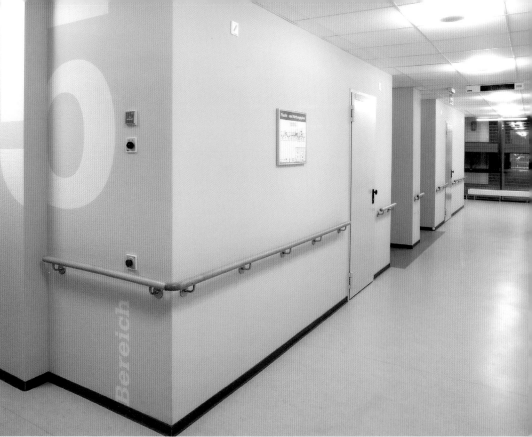

From left to right, from above to below:
Passage, hallway, entrance hall and
reception desk, staircase.
Right: General view.

Von links nach rechts, von oben nach unten:
Übergang, Flur, Eingangshalle mit
Anmeldung, Treppenhaus.
Rechts: Gesamtansicht.

De gauche à droite, de haut en bas:
Passage, couloir, hall d'entrée et
bureau d'informations, escalier.
Droite: Vue d'ensemble.

HELSINGØR PSYCHIATRIC HOSPITAL,
HELSINGØR, DENMARK

PLOT = JDS + BIG

www.jdsarchitects.com
Client: Frederiksborg County, Helsingøer Hospital, **Completion:** 2006, **Gross floor area:** 6,000 m², **Photos:** Vegar Moen, Courtesy of Plot=JDS + BIG.

Left: Light installation first floor. Links: Lichinstallationen der ersten Etage. Gauche: Installations lumineuses au 1er étage. | Right: First floor plan. Rechts: Grundriss erste Etage. Droite: Plan du 1er étage.

As the base of design the architects interviewed patients, personnel and relatives related to the psychiatric hospital. No truth emerged, but a series of paradoxes became evident. The PSY needs to combine the efficiency of a central organization with the freedom and autonomy of a decentralized complex. It needs to allow control and protection while maintaining a free and open atmosphere. In terms of function the PSY is a logistically optimized hospital and in terms of experience it is all but a hospital.

Zu Beginn der Entwurfsarbeit führten die Architekten mit Patienten, Mitarbeitern und Angehörigen Gespräche über die psychiatrische Klinik. Dabei kamen keine neuen Erkenntnisse zutage, sondern eine Reihe von Widersprüchen. Die psychiatrische Klinik braucht die Effizienz einer zentralen Organisation kombiniert mit der Freiheit und Autonomie einer dezentralen Anlage. Sie muss Kontrolle und Schutz gewährleisten und gleichzeitig eine freie und offene Atmosphäre bieten. Funktionell gesehen ist das Projekt eine logistisch optimierte Klinik, von seinem Raumerlebnis her alles andere als ein gewöhnliches Krankenhaus.

Les architectes ont conçu leur projet d'hôpital psychiatrique après avoir interrogé des patients, des familles et le personnel soignant. Cette enquête a mis en évidence un certain nombre de paradoxes. C'est pourquoi le nouvel édifice associe l'efficacité d'une organisation centralisée à l'autonomie d'un complexe décentralisé, l'objectif étant de maintenir un certain contrôle tout en offrant une atmosphère d'ouverture. Cette unité psychiatrique optimise ainsi la logistique tout en minimisant l'aspect purement hospitalier.

ALB HOSPITAL,
MÜNSINGEN, GERMANY

GERHARD KEPPLER WITH
PLANFABRIK SPS AND
WERNER SCHOLDERER

www.keppler-schenk.de, www.planfabrik-sps.de
Client: Distrit Reutlingen, Completion: 2005, Gross floor area: 129,658 sq. ft., Photos: Rüdiger Dempfle.

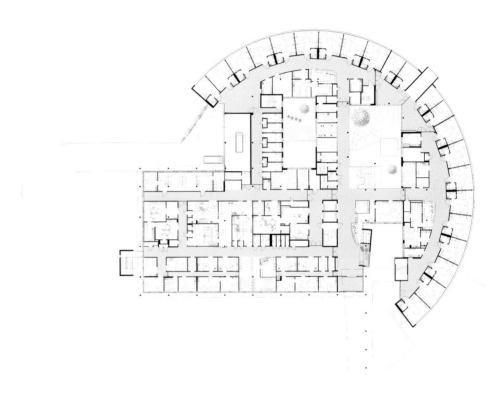

Left: Inner courtyard. Links: Innenhof. Gauche: Cour intérieure. | Right: Ground floor plan. Rechts: Grundriss Erdgeschoss. Droite: Plan du rez-de-chaussée.

The cubic shape of the functional buildings with a technology floor on top is interrupted by a recessed basement, ground and technology floors and changes in the façade. The façade of the three-story, semi-circular nursing building with patients' rooms facing outwards features alternating plaster surfaces and horizontal rows of windows. The ward tract consists of ring segments with a reinforced concrete skeleton frame. Similar to the examination and treatment building, it is based on an orthogonal column grid. The outdoor installations include a freely designed pathway, seating areas, and a therapeutic pathway.

Der kubische Funktionsbau mit aufgesetztem Technikgeschoss wird durch Zurücksetzung des Unter-, Erd- und Technikgeschosses sowie durch wechselnde Fassadengestaltung gegliedert. Der dreigeschossige, halbkreisförmige Pflegebau zeichnet sich durch einen Wechsel von Putzflächen und horizontalen Fensterbändern in der Fassade aus. Das Bettenhaus wurde in Ringsegmenten als Stahlbetonskelett errichtet, der Untersuchungs- und Behandlungsbau beruht auf einem orthogonalen Stützenraster. Die Außenanlage öffnet sich mit frei gestalteten Wegen, Sitznischen und therapeutischem Rundweg zur Alblandschaft hin.

Le rythme de la façade et des zones en retrait au niveau du sous-sol, du rez-de-chaussée et de l'étage technique viennent interrompre l'aspect purement cubique de ces bâtiments fonctionnels. L'immeuble semi-circulaire sur trois niveaux qui abrite les chambres des patients est structuré par des bandes de fenêtres horizontales. Le bâtiment abritant les salles de soins se compose d'un squelette de colonnes en béton armé disposées de manière à former un segment de cercle. À l'extérieur se trouvent une allée au tracé libre, des espaces pourvus de bancs et une allée thérapeutique.

From left to right, from above to below:
Desk in lobby, rear view, atrium.
Right: Ward from southwest.

Von links nach rechts, von oben nach unten:
Empfangstheke, Rückansicht, Atrium.
Rechts: Ansicht Krankenstation aus Südwesten.

De gauche à droite, de haut en bas:
Bureau d'informations, arrière du bâtiment, atrium.
Droite: Pavillon sud-ouest.

CHA WOMEN'S AND CHILDREN'S HOSPITAL,
BUNDANG, KOREA

KMD ARCHITECTS

www.kmdarchitects.com
Client: CHA Health Care System, College of Medicine Pochon CHA University, **Completion:** 2006, **Gross floor area:** 15,330 m², **Photos:** Courtesy of KMD / San Francisco, CA.

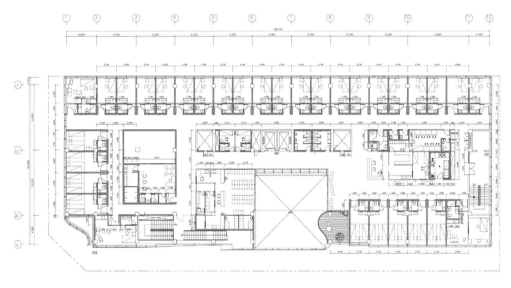

Left: Exterior view. Links: Außenansicht. Gauche: Vue extérieure. | Right: Fourth floor plan. Rechts: Grundriss vierte Etage. Droite: Plan du 4e étage.

Opened in June 2006, the 15330 SM Cha Women's and Children's Hospital in Seoul, Korea serves as another step forward in the evolution of maternity healthcare design. The design reflects the growing body of scientific studies validating the tangible, healing benefits of increased patient exposure to natural elements. Almost two thirds of the hospital's 130 beds are designed as private single-patient suites, incorporating residential furniture, filtered natural light, private Jacuzzi tubs and high-tech multi-media systems. Cha's entire top floor is designed as an innovative onsite full-service spa, a space for relaxation, recovery and rehabilitation.

Das im Juni 2006 eröffnete Frauen- und Kinderkrankenhaus 15330 SM Cha in Seoul, Korea, repräsentiert eine weitere Entwicklungsstufe in der Gestaltung von Entbindungskliniken. Der Entwurf spiegelt die wachsende Anzahl wissenschaftlicher Untersuchungen wider, die den positiven Einfluss eines natürlichen Umfelds auf den Genesungsprozess belegen. Nahezu zwei Drittel der 130 Krankenhausbetten befinden sich in Einbettzimmern mit Wohnmöbeln, gefiltertem Tageslicht, eigenen Jakuzzis und modernsten Multimediasystemen. Chas gesamtes Obergeschoss ist als innovatives Full-Service-Spa konzipiert, als Ort der Entspannung, Erholung und Rehabilitation.

Couvrant une superficie de plus de 15 000 m_, cet hôpital pour femmes et enfants ouvert en juin 2006 inaugure une nouvelle ère en ce qui concerne les services de maternité en Corée du Sud. Les architectes ont pris en compte les nombreuses études soulignant l'importance indiscutable des éléments naturels dans le processus de guérison. Près des deux tiers des cent trente lits sont installés dans des chambres particulières bénéficiant d'un jacuzzi, de meubles de qualité, d'un bon éclairage naturel et d'un équipement multimédia. Le dernier étage est réservé aux services d'hydrothérapie, de relaxation et de rééducation.

From left to right, from above to below:
Detail façade, roof top garden,
spa environment, relaxation area.
Right: Planted atrium.

Von links nach rechts, von oben nach unten:
Fassadendetail, Dachterrassengarten,
Spabereich, Erholungsbereich.
Rechts: Bepflanztes Atrium.

De gauche à droite, de haut en bas:
Détail de la façade, jardin sur toit,
spa, espace de détente.
Droite: Atrium arboré.

PICTOU LANDING HEALTH CENTER,
NEW GLASGOW, NS, CANADA

RICHARD KROEKER, BRIAN LILLEY

Client: Pictou Landing MI'KMAQ First Nation, **Completion:** 2007, **Gross floor area:** 120 m², **Photos:** Paul Toman, Halifax, Richard Kroeker.

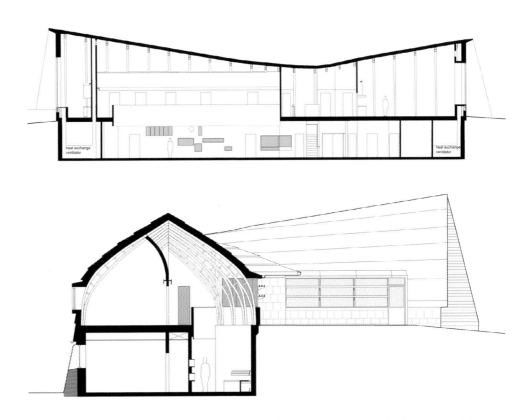

Left: Southwest view. Links: Südwestansicht. Gauche: Vue sud-ouest. | Right: Longsection, cross section. Rechts: Längsschnitt, Querschnitt. Droite: Coupe sur la longueur, coupe transversale.

Pictou Landing First Nation is a community of Mi'kmaq, the indigenous people of the east coast of Canada. The Health Center includes clinics and consultation rooms, administration, and a large community meeting room. Various materials, language, oral traditions, and treaty agreements have defined this culture for many millennia. The Health Center design is based on the indigenous building techniques incorporating local materials and skills. The building bars the north wind and encloses a medicine garden. The interior contributes to the healing process with its natural light, space, and choice of surfaces.

Die Pictou Landing First Nation ist eine Gemeinschaft der Micmac-Indianer an Kanadas Ostküste. Zum Health Center gehören Krankenhaus- und Beratungsräume, Verwaltung und ein großer Versammlungsbereich. Die Kultur der Micmac-Indianer wurde jahrtausendelang von verschiedenen Materialien, Sprachen, mündlichen Überlieferungen und völkerrechtlichen Verträgen geprägt. Der Entwurf der Ambulanz basiert auf den lokalen Bautechniken unter Einsatz von örtlichen Materialien und Fertigkeiten. Das Gebäude hält den Nordwind ab und umschließt einen Arzneigarten. Seine Räumlichkeiten unterstützen mit natürlichem Licht und ausgewählten Oberflächen den Heilungsprozess.

Ce centre de soins est destiné à la nation micmaque qui peuple la côte est du Canada et dont la langue et les traditions sont vieilles de plusieurs milliers d'années. Il se compose d'espaces administratifs, de salles de consultation et de soins ainsi que d'une vaste salle de réunion. Le bâtiment fait une large place aux techniques de construction indigènes et aux matériaux locaux. Il protège du vent du nord le jardin médicinal qui lui est adjacent. La lumière naturelle et les matériaux retenus pour les aménagements intérieurs contribuent au processus de guérison.

From left to right, from above to below:
Community room, interior, waiting area.
Right: Northwest elevation.

Von links nach rechts, von oben nach unten:
Gemeinschaftsraum, Innenansicht, Wartebereich.
Rechts: Nordwestansicht.

De gauche à droite, de haut en bas:
Salle commune, intérieur, salle d'attente.
Droite: Élévation nord-ouest.

CLINIC SAINTE-MARIE,
OSNY, FRANCE

LACOMBE – DE FLORINIER
ARCHITECTS

Client: Association Hospitalière SAINTE MARIE, **Completion:** 1997, **Gross floor area:** 5,374 m², **Photos:** Claude FOULQUIER – Rodez.

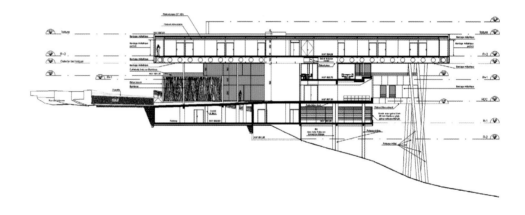

Left: View from valley. Links: Anischt vom Tal. Gauche: Vue depuis l'extérieur. | Right: Section. Rechts: Querschnitt. Droite: Coupe.

The project is built on a steep north-facing plot and consists of a psychiatric clinic (40 bedrooms), a medico-psychological center and an outpatient hospital, positioned around shared technical services. The solution is unique as it positions the bedrooms on the highest floors overlooking the tree tops. The result is a building full of surprises, where the interplay between the stepped volumes and open spaces creates an unconventional environment. The architectural and therapeutic aim was to reach beyond the geometry of urban normality, to help the patients compose a new vision of reality.

Das Projekt an einem steilen, nördlich orientierten Grundstück umfasst eine psychiatrische Klinik, ein medizinisch-psychologisches Zentrum und eine Tagesklinik. Alle Abteilungen sind um gemeinsame Versorgungseinrichtungen angeordnet. Die Lage der Zimmer in den obersten Geschossen mit Blick auf die Baumkronen ist ungewöhnlich. Das Gebäude ist voller Überraschungen, weil die Wechselwirkung zwischen gestuften Volumen und offenen Räumen eine ungewohnte Umgebung schafft. Die Geometrie der städtischen Normalität sollte überwunden werden, um die Patienten bei der Entwicklung neuer Vorstellungen von der Wirklichkeit zu unterstützen.

Ce complexe construit sur un terrain en pente orienté au nord se compose d'une clinique psychiatrique de quarante lits, d'un centre médico-psychologique et d'une unité pour soins externes. Son originalité consiste à avoir placé les chambres des patients au sommet de l'ensemble, de manière à ce qu'elles dominent les arbres du parc. Ce complexe inhabituel et riche en surprises se caractérise par l'interaction des volumes superposés et des espaces ouverts. Tel était bien l'objectif : dépasser la géométrie de la normalité urbaine afin de permettre aux patients de recomposer leur propre image de la réalité.

View fom the reception area. Blick von Rezeption. Vue depuis la réception.

From left to right, from above to below:
Rear view, entrance hall,
façade with bamboo cladding, detail stele.
Right: Terrace.

Von links nach rechts, von oben nach unten:
Rückansicht, Eingangshalle,
Fassade mit Bambusverkleidung, Detail der Steele.
Rechts: Terrasse.

De gauche à droite, de haut en bas:
Arrière du bâtiment, hall d'entrée,
façade et bambous, detail stèles.
Droite: Terrasse.

INNSBRUCK UNIVERSITY CLINICAL CENTER,
INNSBRUCK, AUSTRIA

LOUDON & HABELER ARCHITEKTEN

www.katzberger.at
Client: TILAK – Tyrol Hospital Facilities, Completion: 2001, Gross floor area: 315,645 sq. ft., Photos: Günter Richard Wett.

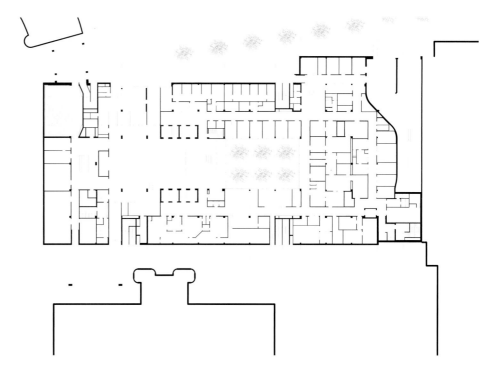

Left: Entrance hall. Links: Eingangshalle. Gauche: Hall d'entrée. | Right: Ground floor plan. Rechts: Grundriss Erdgeschoss. Droite: Plan du rez-de-chaussée.

The wards, including emergency and operative dentistry, neurosurgical operating theaters and internal medicine areas were rebuilt. The wings are illuminated by two-story openings and the terraces have glazed loggias. The new wing is six floors high with several links to the old internal medicine building to the East. A bridge links the third floor with the administrative rooms to the gynecology and neurology clinic. On the façades, Danube lime panels line the lower sectors; while white glass membranes line the upper floors including the six wards and the patients' rooms on the fourth and fifth floor.

Der neue Trakt zählt sechs Geschosse und ist auf mehreren Ebenen mit dem Altbau der Inneren Medizin im Osten verbunden. Neu entstanden Notfallaufnahme, Zahn- und Kieferchirurgie, Neurochirurgische OPs sowie Teile der Inneren Medizin. Eine Brücke führt im dritten Obergeschoss von der Verwaltung zur südlich gelegenen Frauen- und Kopfklinik. Im vierten und fünften Geschoss befinden sich sechs neue Pflegestationen. Zweigeschossige Öffnungen belichten die Trakte, die Terrassen weisen verglaste Loggien auf. Der untere Bereich der Fassaden ist mit Platten aus Donaukalk verkleidet, darüber folgen Membrane aus Weißglas.

L'immeuble d'origine est relié sur plusieurs niveaux à un bâtiment neuf de six étages abritant les urgences, la clinique dentaire, les salles de neurochirurgie et une partie des équipements de médecine générale. Au troisième étage, une passerelle assure la liaison entre les espaces administratifs et les services de gynécologie/neurologie situés au sud du complexe. Six nouvelles unités de soins se trouvent aux quatrième et cinquième étages. L'éclairage intérieur est assuré par des ouvertures sur deux niveaux et des terrasses pourvues de verrières. Des panneaux en calcaire du Danube couvrent le bas des façades, tandis que des plaques en verre blanc sont utilisées aux étages supérieurs.

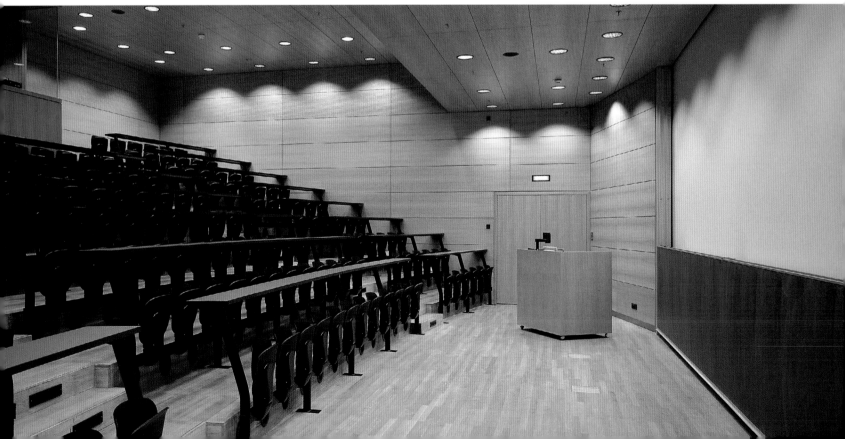

From left to right, from above to below:
Inner courtyard, passage to mezzanine, auditorium.
Right: Entrance hall, main staircase.

Von links nach rechts, von oben nach unten:
Innenhof, Übergang zum Zwischengeschoss, Auditorium.
Rechts: Eingangshalle, Haupttreppe.

De gauche à droite, de haut en bas:
Cour intérieure, couloir menant à la mezzanine, auditorium.
Droite: Hall d'entrée, escalier principal.

KREFELD CLINICAL CENTER,
KREFELD, GERMANY

LUDES ARCHITEKTEN · INGENIEURE

www.ludes.net

Client: Krefeld Clinical Center, Completion: 2005, Gross floor area: 130,734 sq. ft., Photos: Mark Wohlrab.

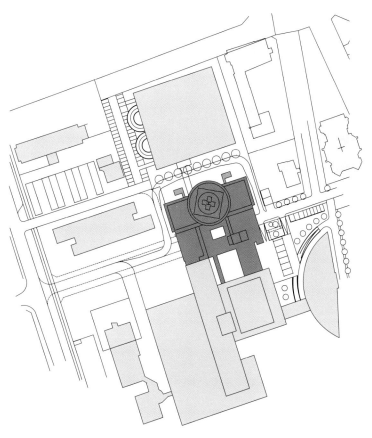

Left: West façade, helipad. Links: Westfassade, Hubschrauberlandeplatz. Gauche: Façade ouest, aire d'atterrissage pour hélicoptères. |
Right: Site plan. Rechts: Lageplan. Droite: Plan du site.

The new high-tech operating theater center contains 18 operating theaters plus zones and rooms extending across two floors. The design focused on the efficient use of space and short distances between the rooms. The transition area to the operating theaters was also redesigned to ensure rapid admission of patients. The holding area with a recovery room is illuminated by daylight. Additional elements link some areas; e.g. an elevator links the helicopter landing pad on the roof and the patient delivery on the ground floor. The building's façade features enclosed wall surfaces and transparent glass elements.

Auf zwei Ebenen werden 18 OP-Säle in Clustern mit separaten Instrumentier- und Einleitungszonen angeordnet. Dies ermöglicht eine Parallelisierung der Teilprozesse mit hoher Effizienz und optimierten Funktionsabläufen. Eine natürlich belichteter kombinierter Holding-/Aufwachbereich ermöglicht eine zeitnahe, kurzwegige Zuführung der Patienten zum OP. Ein Aufzugsknoten verknüpft Hubschrauberlandeplatz und Notfallaufnahme mit den OP-Ebenen. Das High-Tech-Gebäude, bekrönt durch den Landeplatz, veranschaulicht in besonderer Weise den medizinischen Anspruch und die fachliche Kompetenz der Klinik.

Ce nouveau centre de chirurgie high-tech se compose de dix-huit blocs opératoires et de leurs espaces annexes répartis sur deux niveaux. Les architectes ont cherché à optimiser l'utilisation de l'espace, à minimiser les déplacements internes, et à accélérer l'accès des patients aux blocs opératoires. La salle de réanimation dispose d'un éclairage naturel. Un ascenseur assure la liaison entre la passerelle d'hélicoptère et le rez-de-chaussée. La façade combine des éléments opaques et des bandes vitrées.

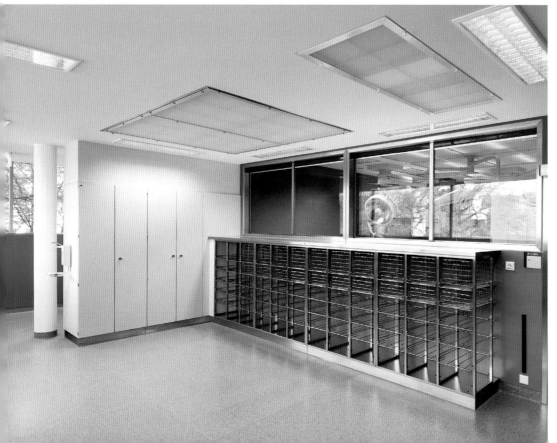

From left to right, from above to below:
Central washing area, holding area,
equipment area, anasthesia space.
Right: Anesthetic recovery area.

Von links nach rechts, von oben nach unten:
Zentrale Waschzone, Holding-Area,
Sterilgutversorgung, Arbeitsbereich Aufwachraum.
Rechts: Holding-Area.

De gauche à droite, de haut en bas:
Sanitaires, espace d'accueil,
salle du matériel, salle d'anesthésie.
Droite: Salle de réveil.

MINAMIGAOKA CLINIC,
SAGA, JAPAN

MATSUYAMA ARCHITECT AND ASSOCIATES

www.matsuyama-a.co.jp
Client: Hirofumi Hayashi, **Completion:** 2005, **Gross floor area:** 982,740 m², **Photos:** Toshihisa Ishii.

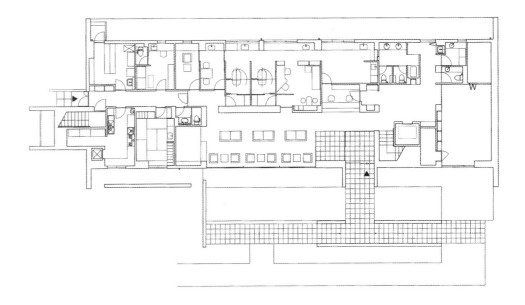

Left: Façade by night. Links: Fassade bei Nacht. Gauche: Façade de nuit. | **Right:** Floor plan. Rechts: Grundriss. Droite: Plan.

The building is dominated by the play of light in the changing seasons. Resembling a box, the hospital measures 34 m x 10 m and contains all equipments and services of a hospital. Examination and patients' rooms are on the first floor, while the waiting room is on the ground floor. A reflecting pool and a terrace offer patients and visitors opportunities for rest and relaxation. Inside, the combination of a symmetrical design with natural materials creates a gentle flowing interior.

Das Gebäude wird bestimmt von der Dominanz des Lichtes im Wechsel der Jahreszeiten. Die Klinik, dessen Erscheinung einer Box gleicht, ist auf 34 x 10 Meter angelegt und beherbergt alle Einrichtungen und Leistungen eines Krankenhauses. Untersuchungsräume und Patientenzimmer sind in der ersten Etage zu finden, während sich im Erdgeschoss das Wartezimmer befindet. Ein spiegelnder Pool und eine Terrasse sorgen im Außenbereich für Ruhe und Entspannung der Patienten und Besucher. Die Verbindung von symmetrischem Design und natürlichen Materialien erzeugt ein sanftes, fließendes Interieur.

Cette clinique se caractérise par une lumière différente à chaque saison. Il s'agit d'un bâtiment orthogonal de trente-quatre mètres sur quarante, qui offre une gamme complète des services hospitaliers. L'accueil et la salle d'attente se trouvent au rez-de-chaussée, les chambres et les salles de soins au premier étage. À l'extérieur, une terrasse et un plan d'eau créent une atmosphère agréable et calme. Le design linéaire de l'aménagement intérieur utilise des matériaux naturels, avec pour résultat un ensemble à la fois paisible et fluide.

From left to right, from above to below:
Approach to entrance, waiting room,
general view of the façade, reflecting pool.
Right: Terrace.

Von links nach rechts, von oben nach unten:
Zufahrt zum Eingang, Warterzimmer,
Gesamtansicht der Fassade, spiegelnder Pool.
Rechts: Terrasse.

De gauche à droite, de haut en bas:
Passage vers l'entrée, salle d'attente, vue d'ensemble
de la façade, bassin avec installations lumineuses.
Droite: Terrasse.

ST. OLAV'S HOSPITAL NEURO CENTER,
TRONDHEIM, NORWAY

NARUD – STOKKE – WIIG AS

www.nsw.no
Client: Helsebygg midt-Norge (HBMN), **Completion:** 2005, **Gross floor area:** 31,000 m², **Photos:** Grethe Britt Fredriksen.

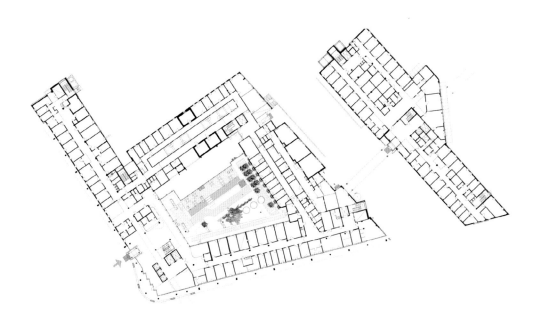

Left: **Street side view.** Links: Straßenansicht. Gauche: Vue depuis la rue. | Right: **First floor plan.** Rechts: Grundriss erste Etage. Droite: Plan du 1er étage.

Frisk Arch, a collaboration between Narud Stokke Wiig Arch. Ltd. and Nils Torp Arch. Ltd., won the competition for the new Trondheim University Hospital in 1995. The project focused on three qualities –organization based on decentralized hospital units, full operation of the hospital during the construction period, and an urban plan based on the block structure of this part of Trondheim. As hospital buildings are very complex, easy orientation was another priority. Simple communication patterns, emphasized by color, and material schemes as well as art installations guided the interior design.

Frisk Arch, eine Kooperation zwischen Narud Stokke Wiig Arch. Ltd. und Nils Torp Arch. Ltd., gewann 1995 den Wettbewerb für die neue Universitätsklinik Trondheim. Wesentlich für das Projekt waren eine auf dezentralen Klinikeinheiten basierende Organisation, ein uneingeschränkter Krankenhausbetrieb während der Bauphase und die Blockstruktur in diesem Teil Trondheims als Grundlage. Die sehr komplexen Krankenhausbauten erforderten zudem eine leichte Orientierung. Einfache Kommunikationsmuster, unterstützt von Farbe und Materialkonzepten ebenso wie von Kunstinstallationen, bestimmten die Innengestaltung.

En 1995, le bureau Frisk Arch – auquel collaborent Nils Torp Arch. Ltd et Narud Stokke Wiig Arch. Ltd – a été lauréat du concours visant à l'agrandissement du CHU de Trondheim. Le projet retenu s'articule selon trois axes principaux : organisation en unités décentralisées, non-interruption de l'activité des structures préexistantes durant les travaux, et intégration dans le tissu urbain traditionnel de cette partie de la ville. Par ailleurs, les architectes ont cherché à faciliter l'orientation à l'intérieur de l'hôpital, ce qui est absolument nécessaire dans ce type d'environnement complexe. C'est pourquoi les aménagements intérieurs utilisent des schémas de communication simples à base de couleurs, de matériaux diversifiés et d'installations artistiques.

From left to right, from above to below:
Courtyard, lobby, view above reception, main staircase.
Right: Courtyard.

Von links nach rechts, von oben nach unten:
Innenhof, Lobby, Blick auf die Anmeldung, Haupttreppe.
Rechts: Innenhof.

De gauche à droite, de haut en bas:
Cour intérieure, hall, vue sur la réception, escalier principal.
Droite: Cour intérieure.

ANGELIKA-LAUTENSCHLÄGER-CLINIC, CENTER FOR PEDIATRICS, UNIVERSITY CLINICAL CENTER,
HEIDELBERG, GERMANY

NICKL & PARTNER ARCHITEKTEN

www.nickl-partner.com
Client: State of Baden-Württemberg represented by Vermögen und Bau Baden-Württemberg, Universitäts-bauamt Heidelberg, **Completion:** 2008, **Gross floor area:** 19,900 m², **Photos:** Stefan Müller, Munich.

Left: Library. Links: Bibliothek. Gauche: Bibliothèque. | Right: Floor plan. Rechts: Grundriss. Droite: Plan.

The design is based on the magic cube concept. The outer skin consists of suspended glass sheets and continues downwards with entwined greenery. The corners of the cube are specially designed and connected via two inner courtyards. These contain, for example, the library and the children's planet, the child care facility for siblings. The colors dominate the patient floors up to the patients' cupboard. The hospital consists of four units – the care cube, the entrance hall, the functional building, and the parents' guest house. The four structures form a square surrounding a garden for patients.

Die Klinik variiert das Thema des Zauberwürfels. Vorgehängte Gläser bilden als farbige Streifen die Außenhaut, die sich mit einer Berankung nach unten fortsetzt. Die Ecken des Würfels sind besonders ausgeformt und über zwei Innenhöfe verbunden. Hier finden sich etwa die Bibliothek und der Kinderpla-net, die Betreuungseinrichtung für Geschwister. Die Farben prägen die Pflegegeschosse bis hin zu den Patientenschränken. Die Klinik gliedert sich in vier Baukörper: den Pflegekubus, die Eingangshalle, den Funktionsbau und das Elterngästehaus. Die vier Kör-per wiederum umschließen einen Patientengarten und bilden ein Quadrat.

Cette clinique se compose de plusieurs « cubes magiques ». Des plaques de verre de différentes couleurs forment une enveloppe extérieure bordée au niveau du sol par des espaces végétaux. La cli-nique intègre notamment une bibliothèque, un es-pace de jeux pour enfants et des services destinés aux frères et sœurs. Diverses couleurs caractérisent les espaces réservés aux patients. L'ensemble se compose de quatre volumes différents : le cube des soins, le hall d'entrée, le bâtiment fonctionnel et celui abritant les chambres réservées aux parents. Ces quatre volumes sont groupés en carré autour d'un jardin accessible aux patients.

Entrance view and reception. Blick auf den Eingang und Anmeldung. Vue sur l'entrée et la réception.

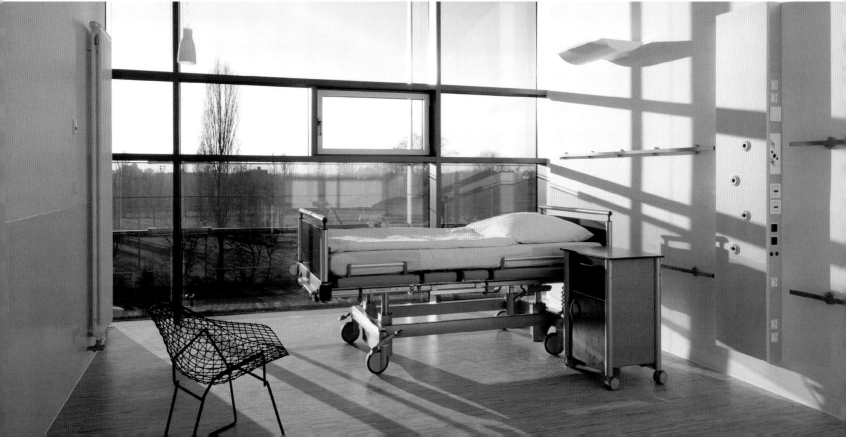

From left to right, from above to below:
Staircase, ornamental work at passage, patient room.
Right: Playground.

Von links nach rechts, von oben nach unten:
Treppenhaus, Kunst am Übergang, Patientenzimmer.
Rechts: Kinderspielplatz.

De gauche à droite, de haut en bas:
Escalier, installations artistiques vers l'entrée, chambre des
patients.
Droite: Aire de jeux pour enfants.

AGATHARIED HOSPITAL,
AGATHARIED, GERMANY

NICKL & PARTNER ARCHITEKTEN

www.nickl-partner.com

Client: District of Miesbach and District of Upper Bavaria, **Completion:** 1998, **Gross floor area:** 46,200 m², **Photos:** Stefan Müller-Naumann, Munich.

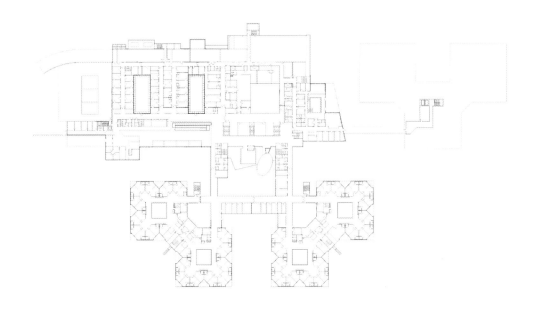

Left: Pavilion. Links: Pavilion. Gauche: Pavillon. | Right: First floor plan. Rechts: Grundriss erste Etage. Droite: Plan du 1er étage.

Full glazing on the sidewalls illuminates the rooms, while lamellas function like translucent curtains. From the entrance hall, four connected walkways lead to the wards and psychiatric department. The layout of the wards keeps hospital staff as close to the patients as possible. The rooms are diagonal from the courtyard and the external shape allowing the addition of a glazed conservatory in front of each room, which can be used year-round to improve the airflow into the rooms. The controlled fresh air circulation buffers the ward temperature levels, resulting in a healing aura.

Raumhohe Verglasungen an der Längsseite sorgen für einen lichtdurchfluteten Raum, gleichzeitig wirken Lamellen wie ein transluzenter Vorhang. Von der Eingangshalle führen aufgestelzte Verbindungsbauten in die Bettenhäuser und die Psychiatrie. Der Grundriss hält die Wege vom Pflegenden zum Patienten so kurz wie möglich. Zum Innenhof sind die Zimmer diagonal gestellt. Dadurch entstehen vor den Krankenzimmern einfach verglaste Wintergärten, die ganzjährig zur Klimaverbesserung genutzt werden. Durch die gesteuerte Frischluftzirkulation werden Klimaspitzen abgepuffert: ein heilsames Klima entsteht.

Une façade entièrement vitrée garnie de stores donne au bâtiment un aspect translucide. Derrière le hall d'entrée se trouvent deux bâtiments surélevés : l'un abrite les chambres, l'autre les services psychiatriques. Les architectes ont cherché à réduire au minimum les déplacements du personnel soignant. Les chambres sont positionnées en diagonale par rapport à la cour intérieure dont les plantes améliorent l'air ambiant été comme hiver. Un système de ventilation assure une climatisation naturelle qui contribue au processus de guérison.

Entrance hall. Eingangshalle. Hall d'entrée.

From left to right, from above to below:
Nurse station, glazed façade of entrance hall.
Right: View onto entrance hall.

Von links nach rechts, von oben nach unten:
Schwesternstützpunkt, verglaste Fassade der Eingangshalle.
Rechts: Blick auf die Eingangshalle.

De gauche à droite, de haut en bas:
Service des infirmières, façade vitrée du hall d'entrée.
Droite: Vue sur le hall d'entrée.

CLINICAL CENTER OF THE
JOHANN WOLFGANG GOETHE-UNIVERSITY
FRANKFURT / MAIN, GERMANY

NICKL & PARTNER ARCHITEKTEN

www.nickl-partner.com

Client: State of Hessen represented by Hessisches Baumanagement, Regionalniederlassung Rhein-Main, **Completion:** 1st phase East: 2007, initiation of all buildings: 2011, **Gross floor area:** 19,900 m², **Photos:** Stefan Müller-Naumann, Munich.

Left: East façade with helipad. Links: Ostfassade mit Hubschrauberlandeplatz. Gauche: Façade est avec aire d'atterrissage. | Right: Floor plan. Rechts: Grundriss. Droite: Plan.

The aim of the reconstruction and expansion of the Frankfurt university hospital was to structure and enlarge the premises in compliance with the new requirements and to equip it for today's demands in terms of technology, functionality and design. The building plan focused on the patient instead of the technology. The urban planning design creates a connection to the river and the city. The projecting roof connects the annex to the core building and marks the new building entrance over the central hall, which is the connection point between the university and the hospital.

Mit dem Umbau und der Erweiterung der Universitätsklinik Frankfurt sollten die Baulichkeiten entsprechend den neuen Erfordernissen strukturiert und vergrößert werden. Außerdem war die Klinik technisch, funktionell und gestalterisch auf den heutigen Stand zu bringen. Dabei konzentrierte sich der Bauplan auf den Patienten und nicht auf die Technik. Die städtebauliche Gestaltung ermöglicht eine Verbindung zum Fluss und zur Stadt. Das vorspringende Dach vermittelt zwischen dem Anbau und dem Hauptgebäude und markiert den neuen Gebäudezugang zu der zentralen Eingangshalle, dem Verbindungspunkt zwischen Universität und Klinik.

Les travaux de modernisation et d'agrandissement du CHU de Francfort visaient à satisfaire aux exigences actuelles en matière de technologie médicale, de fonctionnalité et de design, tout en accordant la priorité aux patients plutôt qu'à la technique. Le CHU est maintenant relié à la fois à la ville et aux berges de la rivière. Le nouveau hall d'entrée, qui assure la liaison entre l'hôpital proprement dit et les bâtiments universitaires, se caractérise par un toit en surplomb.

Reception area in lobby. Eingangshalle mit Empfangsbereich. Réception dans le hall d'accueil.

From left to right, from above to below:
Detail artificial, canopy main entrance,
hallway first floor, entrance area,
Right: Interior entrance hall.

Von links nach rechts, von oben nach unten:
Kunst am Bau, Vordach Haupteingangsbereich,
Flur erste Etage, Eingangshalle.
Rechts: Eingangshalle Innenansicht.

De gauche à droite, de haut en bas:
Détail artistique, entrée principale avec toit avant,
couloir du 1er étage, hall d'entrée.
Droite: Hall d'entrée.

CLINIC HANOVER NORDSTADT,
HANOVER, GERMANY

Haus T

NICKL & PARTNER ARCHITEKTEN

www.nickl-partner.com
Client: Clinic Hanover, **Completion:** phase A: 2008, phase B: 2010, **Gross floor area:** 29,900 m², **Photos:** Stefan Müller-Naumann, Munich.

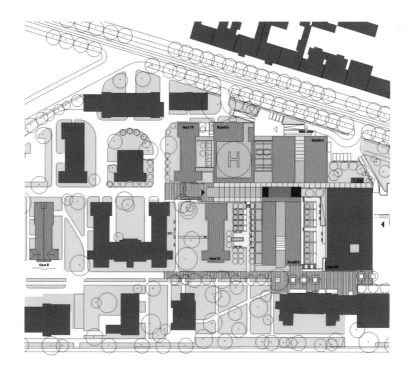

Left: Entrance area. Links: Eingangsbereich. Gauche: Entrée. | Right: Site plan. Rechts: Lageplan. Droite: Plan du site.

The new construction incorporates the entire structure of the landmarked extended building, which distinguishes the hospital complex. On the one hand, maintaining the character of the pavilion-style individual buildings preserves the park landscape, while on the other hand the transparent access building combines the structures into a functional, clearly-structured and connected unit. The scale and limited size of each unit, coupled with optimal lighting, support the healing process.

Der Neubau der Klinik nimmt die Gesamtstruktur der längsgerichteten denkmalgeschützten Riegel auf, die das Klinik-Ensemble prägt. Mittels der Beibehaltung des Charakters der pavillonartigen Einzelhausbebauung bleibt einesteils die Parklandschaft erhalten; andererseits bindet das transparente Erschließungsgebäude die Baukörper zu einer funktionalen Einheit der Übersichtlichkeit und kurzen Wege zusammen. Die Maßstäblichkeit und überschaubare Größe jeder Einheit unterstützt, flankiert von optimaler Belichtung, den Heilungsprozess.

Les nouveaux bâtiments intègrent la forme allongée de la barre classée monument historique qui caractérise ce complexe hospitalier. Par ailleurs, ils tiennent compte de la répartition en différents pavillons à l'intérieur d'un parc, tandis que le hall d'accès transparent les unifie en optimisant les distances. Les dimensions humaines de chacun des pavillons, associées à un bon éclairage naturel, contribuent au processus de guérison.

View toward entrance. Ansicht Eingangsbereich. Vue sur l'entrée.

From left to right, from above to below:
Reception at entrance area, detail façade,
children's medical unit.
Right: Detail façade.

Von links nach rechts, von oben nach unten:
Empfang im Eingangsbereich,
Fassadendetail, Kinderstation.
Rechts: Fassadendetail.

SOPHIEN AND HUFELAND CLINIC,
WEIMAR, GERMANY

CARLOS OTT, ALBERTO BORNES

www.carlosott.com

Client: Sophien- und Hufeland Klinikum GmbH, formerly Krankenhaus Neubau Weimar GmbH, **Completion:** 1998, **Gross floor area:** 622,132 sq. ft., **Photos:** Siegfried Falke.

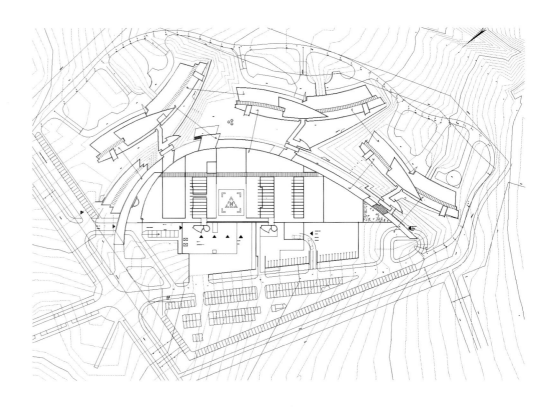

Left: Main entrance. Links: Haupteingang. Gauche: Entrée principale. | Right: Site plan. Rechts: Lageplan. Droite: Plan du site.

The strict geometric architecture of the surgical and operating theater wings is counterbalanced by the flowing form of the ward tract. The arched and glazed main corridor with an admission point, waiting areas, a chapel, cafeteria, shops, library and multifunctional spaces is a central communication room for patients, visitors and staff. The examination and treatment area is located on one floor, enhanced by nuclear medicine facilities, computer and nuclear resonance scanning, and a central laboratory. The roof of the operating theater and diagnosis center also functions as a helicopter-landing pad.

Die streng geometrische Architektur des Funktions- und OP-Traktes wird durch die fließende Form der Bettenhäuser abgemildert. Die vollverglaste, bogenförmige Verbindungsmagistrale mit Aufnahme, Wartezonen, Kapelle, Cafeteria, Ladengeschäften und Bibliothek stellt einen zentralen Kommunikationsraum für Patienten, Besucher und Personal dar. Der Untersuchungs- und Behandlungsbereich ist auf einer Ebene konzentriert und wird ergänzt durch ein Zentrallabor, nuklearmedizinische Einrichtungen sowie Computer- und Kerntomographie. Das Dach des OP- und Diagnosezentrums dient als Hubschrauberlandeplatz.

La géométrie stricte de l'aile abritant les salles d'opération contraste avec les formes fluides du bâtiment où se trouvent les diverses salles de soins. L'espace vitré qui abrite l'accueil, les salles d'attente, la chapelle, la cafétéria, la bibliothèque et diverses boutiques favorise la communication entre les patients, les visiteurs et le personnel médical. Toutes les salles de consultation et de soins — notamment les scanners, le laboratoire central et les salles de médecine nucléaire — sont regroupés au même niveau. Une plate-forme pour hélicoptère est aménagée sur le toit du bâtiment abritant les salles d'opération et le centre de diagnostic.

From left to right, from above to below:
Detail main corridor, aerial view, courtyard, façade.
Right: Ward tracts.

Von links nach rechts, von oben nach unten:
Detailansicht des Hauptgangs, Luftbild, Innenhof, Fassade.
Rechts: Krankenstationen.

De gauche à droite, de haut en bas:
Accès principal, vue aérienne, cour intérieure, façade.
Droite: Service des soins.

www.pargade.com
Client: Pôle de Sante Sarthe et Loire, Completion: 2007, Gross floor area: 34,000 m², Photos: Fessy (212 b.), Marchand et Meffre (210, 212 a.l., 212 a.r., 213).

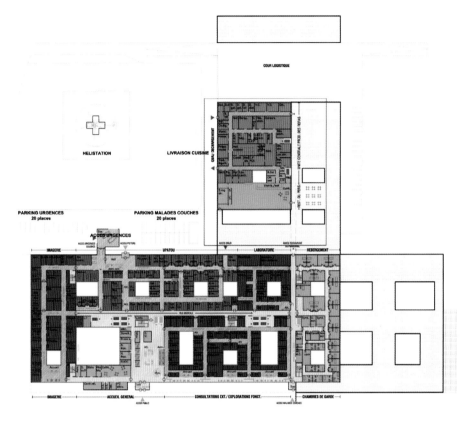

Left: Patio and façade. Links: Innenhof und Fassade. Gauche: Cour extérieure et façade. | Right: Ground floor plan. Rechts: Grundriss Erdgeschoss Droite: Plan du rez-de-chaussée.

With only 300 beds on three different levels, this hospital has human dimensions. Overlooking a valley, it features a technologically sophisticated architecture that strongly contrasts with the rural setting. High vertical windows structure the façade of printed glass. The horizontal succession of the various functions leads to increased transparency, facilitates communications within the building and is compatible with a future extension. Color plays an important role in the green courtyards, where different kinds of materials structure the space and underscore the importance of art within the hospital.

Mit nur 300 Betten auf drei verschiedenen Ebenen bleibt dieses über einem Tal gebaute Krankenhaus patientenfreundlich. Die Hightech-Architektur bildet einen starken Kontrast zum ländlichen Hintergrund. Hohe Fenster beleben die Fassade aus bedruckten Glasplatten. Die waagerechte Folge der verschiedenen Funktionen sorgt für Transparenz, vereinfacht die Kommunikation innerhalb des Gebäudes und ermöglicht eine zukünftige Erweiterung. In den begrünten Höfen spielt die Farbe eine besondere Rolle: Materialien aus verschiedenen Farbtönen strukturieren den Raum und unterstreichen die Bedeutung der Kunst in diesem Krankenhaus.

Le nouvel hôpital de trois cents lits répartis sur trois niveaux a une taille humaine. Dominant un vallon, il crée un contraste entre la rusticité du paysage et le raffinement technologique de son architecture. De hautes fenêtres structurent la façade en verre sérigraphié. La juxtaposition horizontale des pôles d'activité offre une grande visibilité, facilite la circulation à l'intérieur du bâtiment et permettra des agrandissements ultérieurs. La couleur joue un rôle important dans les cours plantées d'arbres : les teintes des différents matériaux y structurent l'espace et soulignent l'apport essentiel de l'art à cet hôpital.

From left to right, from above to below:
Reflections of façade, pink corridor, reception in hall.
Right: Pink patio.

Von links nach rechts, von oben nach unten:
Spiegelung der Fassade, pinkfarbener Flur, Empfang im Eingangs-
bereich.
Rechts: Pinkfarbener Innenhof.

De gauche à droite, de haut en bas:
Reflets sur la façade, couloir rose, réception dans le hall.
Droite: Patio rose.

PARKIN ARCHITECTS LIMITED AND ADAMSON ASSOCIATES ARCHITECTS

www.parkin.ca
Client: William Osler Health Center, **Completion:** 2007, **Gross floor area:** 1,200,000 sq. ft.,
Photos: Toronto On, Adamson Associates.

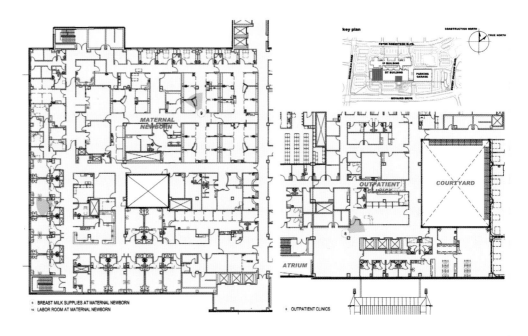

Left: Glazed façade. Links: Verglaste Fassade. Gauche: Façade vitrée. | Right: Floor plan. Rechts: Grundriss. Droite: Plan.

With a total area of 111,484 m², 608 acute care beds and 18 operating theaters, this hospital will replace the existing Brampton Memorial Hospital as the most important acute care hospital of the region. Parkin's design consists of a three-floor building for diagnosis and treatment as well as a six-floor patient ward block. Both buildings are connected at all levels by two groups of corridors. Upon completion, the facility will feature 37 departments ranging from treatment and diagnosis up to emergency wards and out-patient care.

Die 111 484 m² große Einrichtung mit 608 Akutbetten und 18 OP-Sälen wird das bestehende Brampton Memorial Hospital als wichtigstes Akutkrankenhaus der Region ablösen. Parkins Entwurf enthält ein dreigeschossiges Gebäude für Diagnostik und Behandlung sowie ein sechsgeschossiges Bettenhaus. Beide Bauten sind auf jeder Ebene von zwei Gruppen mit Korridoren miteinander verbunden. Bei Fertigstellung wird die Einrichtung über 37 Abteilungen verfügen, die von der Behandlung und Diagnostik bis zur Notaufnahme und ambulanten Versorgung reichen.

Il s'agit ici d'un des premiers hôpitaux AFP de l'Ontario (Alternative Financing and Procurement), construit en seulement deux ans. Afin de mieux intégrer le bâtiment au tissu urbain et de lui donner un aspect plus engageant, les architectes ont choisi de le construire à proximité de la rue. Le complexe hospitalier se compose d'un bâtiment de trois étages pour soins externes et hospitalisation, ainsi que d'un immeuble de sept étages qui abrite un institut de recherche sur la santé mentale doté d'un auditorium de deux cents places et de divers équipements éducatifs.

Exterior view by night. Außenansicht am Abend. Vue extérieure de nuit.

From left to right, from above to below:
Atrium, main lobby, north side main entrance, patient room.
Right: Intensive care.

Von links nach rechts, von oben nach unten:
Atrium, Hauptlobby, nördlicher Haupteingang, Patientenzimmer.
Rechts: Intensivstation.

De gauche à droite, de haut en bas:
Atrium, hall principal, entrée principale nord, chambre des
patients.
Droite: Service des soins intensifs.

ROYAL OTTAWA HOSPITAL,
OTTAWA, ON, CANADA

PARKIN ARCHITECTS LIMITED, ADAMSON ASSOCIATES ARCHITECTS AND BRISBIN BROOK BEYNON, ARCHITECTS

www.parkin.ca

Client: Ellis Don Corporation, Completion: 2006, Gross floor area: 400,000 sq. ft., Renderings: Toronto On, Adamson Associates.

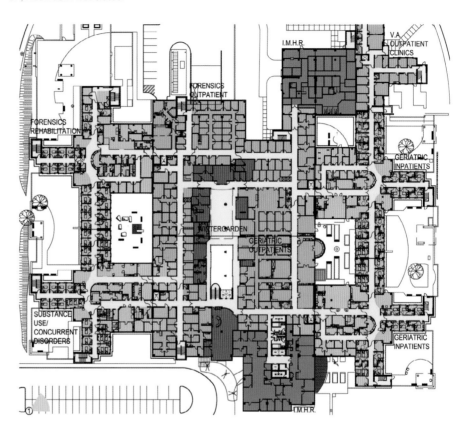

Left: General view. Links: Gesamtansicht. Gauche: Vue d'ensemble. | Right: First floor plan. Rechts: Grundriss erste Etage. Droite: Plan du 1er étage.

The proposed 1.2 million square-feet facility will replace the existing Brampton Memorial Hospital as the primary acute care facility for the area, with 608 acute-care beds and 18 operating rooms. The Parkin design includes a three-story Diagnostics and Treatment Building, as well as a six-story Inpatient Building linked via two sets of corridors at each level. When completed, the facility will have a total of 37 departments, ranging from surgery and diagnostic services to emergency and ambulatory care.

Als eine der ersten medizinischen Versorgungsein-richtungen in Ontario mit alternativer Finanzierung musste das Krankenhaus innerhalb einer Frist von zwei Jahren fertiggestellt sein. Um es in der Allge-meinheit bewusst zu machen und ein für Passanten positives und einladendes Erscheinungsbild zu schaf-fen, platzierte Parkin den Neubau näher zur Straße in einen Bereich vor und neben den vorhandenen Gebäuden. Der Bau umfasst eine dreigeschossige Einrichtung für stationäre und ambulante Versorgung sowie einen siebengeschossigen Turm für das Insti-tute for Mental Health Research, das einen Hörsaal und ein Ausbildungszentrum beherbergt.

Cet hôpital d'une surface totale d'environ 360 000 m_ remplace une structure plus ancienne. Avec dix-huit salles d'opération et 608 lits au total, c'est le plus important centre de soins intensifs de la région de Brampton. Il se compose d'un bâtiment de trois étages pour les diagnostics et le traitement, auquel s'ajoute un immeuble de six étages réservé aux patients hospitalisés, les deux entités étant reliées entre elles à plusieurs niveaux. Le nouvel hôpital propose trente-sept services différents, notamment la chirurgie, les urgences, le diagnostic et les soins externes.

From left to right, from above to below:
Library, chapel, atrium.
Right: Lounge in atrium.

Von links nach rechts, von oben nach unten:
Bibliothek, Kapelle, Atrium.
Rechts: Aufenthaltsraum im Atrium.

De gauche à droite, de haut en bas:
Bibliothèque, chapelle, atrium.
Droite: Hall dans l'atrium.

BELLEVUE HOSPITAL AMBULATORY CARE BUILDING,

NEW YORK CITY, NY, USA

PEI COBB FREED & PARTNERS
ARCHITECTS

www.pcf-p.com
Client: Dormitory Authority of the State of New York, **Completion:** 2005, **Gross floor area:** 210,000 sq. ft.,
Photos: Paul Warchol, Pei Cobb Freed & Partners Architects LLP.

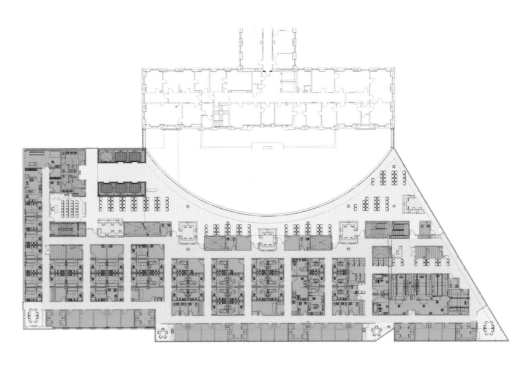

Left: Entrance hall. Links: Eingangshalle. Gauche: Hall d'entrée. | Right: Floor plan. Rechts: Grundriss. Droite: Plan.

The new building serves as the main entrance for the entire hospital complex, also increasing the needed medical space. In reintroducing the McKim, Mead and White architecture, the challenge was combining old and new. The glazed atrium has become the emblematic heart of Bellevue. Visitors enter through glass entrances, the wide steps and ramp provide access to the atrium, with the striking view of the brick wall rising through a sloped skylight to its culmination. The conjunction of the sweeping, curved balconies of the new building and the handsome historic brickwork is celebrated in natural light.

Der Neubau fungiert als Haupteingang für den gesamten Krankenhauskomplex und erweitert außerdem die Flächen für die medizinische Versorgung. Da die Architektur von McKim, Mead und White einzubinden war, lag die Herausforderung in einer Kombination von Neu und Alt. Aus dem gläsernen Atrium wurde das zeichenhafte Herzstück des Bellevue. Besucher gelangen dorthin über Glaseingänge, Stufen und Rampen. Dabei sehen sie, wie die eindrucksvolle Backsteinwand durch ein schräges Oberlicht bis zu ihrem höchsten Punkt aufsteigt. Die Verbindung der geschwungenen Balkone des Neubaus mit dem historischen Mauerwerk kommt besonders bei Tageslicht zur Geltung.

La difficulté consistait ici à faire du neuf avec du vieux. La grande verrière, très réussie, caractérise l'hôpital de Bellevue après les récents travaux de modernisation et d'agrandissement. On y accède par un large escalier et une rampe, pour découvrir une vue surprenante sur la façade du bâtiment ancien. L'abondante lumière naturelle met en valeur les briques traditionnelles et les audacieuses formes incurvées de l'architecture moderne.

From left to right, from above to below:
Glazed roof, atrium with view toward wards, interior.
Right: Reception in entrance hall.

Von links nach rechts, von oben nach unten:
Verglastes Dach, Atrium mit Blick auf die Stationen, Innenansicht.
Rechts: Anmeldung in Eingangshalle.

De gauche à droite, de haut en bas:
Plafond vitré, atrium avec vue sur les services, intérieur.
Droite: Réception dans le hall d'entrée.

UNIVERSITY CLINICAL CENTER,
HALLE-KRÖLLWITZ, GERMANY

PLANUNGSGESELLSCHAFT UKK
HASCHER +JEHLE ARCHITECTS
AND ENGINEERS MONNERJAN
KAST WALTER ARCHITECTS

www.hascherjehle.de
Client: Martin Luther University Halle-Wittenberg, **Completion:** 2003, **Gross floor area:** 693,912 sq. ft.,
Photos: Jörg F. Müller.

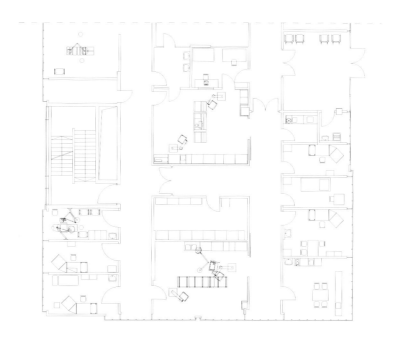

Left: Street side view with helipad. Links: Straßenansicht mit Hubschrauberlandeplatz. Gauche: Vue depuis la rue et aire d'atterrissage. |
Right: Ground floor plan. Rechts: Grundriss Erdgeschoss. Droite: Plan du rez-de-chaussée.

With mostly naturally illuminated and ventilated rooms, the eight new buildings are linked to the landscape and structured by a central main corridor. The entrance hall, offering services and a link to public transportation, is located in the western part of the complex. The radionuclide laboratory with an upstream lock and laboratories with the latest safety regulations for gene technology are located at the eastern edge. The new development was designed in functional column grids allowing the flexible use of the clinic and operating theater areas and facilitating their later use for other purposes.

Die acht neuen Teilbauten sind mit der umgebenden Landschaft verbunden und durch die zentrale Magistrale gegliedert. Im Westen des Komplexes liegt die Eingangshalle mit umfassenden Serviceleistungen und direkter Anbindung an das öffentliche Nahverkehrsnetz. Am Ostrand der Neubebauung befindet sich das Radionuklid-Labor mit vorgeschalteter Schleuse sowie Labore, die nach den neuesten Sicherheitsbestimmungen für Gentechnik eingerichtet wurden. Der gesamte Neubau wurde in funktionalen Stützenrastern ausgeführt und so die flexible Nutzung der Klinik- und OP-Bereiche sowie spätere Umnutzungen ermöglicht.

Huit bâtiments qui privilégient la ventilation et l'éclairage naturels sont reliés entre eux par un couloir central et s'intègrent bien dans l'environnement. Le hall d'entrée, pourvu de divers services et d'un accès aux transports en commun, est situé à l'ouest du complexe, où se trouvent également les installations radio-nucléaires et des laboratoires ultramodernes de génie génétique. Une structure porteuse à base de colonnes garantit une utilisation flexible des espaces cliniques et des salles d'opération, qui pourront éventuellement recevoir d'autres affectations à l'avenir.

From left to right, from above to below:
Ward track, detail façade, atrium.
Right: View onto entrance area.

Von links nach rechts, von oben nach unten:
Stationsflur, Fassadendetail, Atrium.
Rechts: Blick auf den Eingansbereich.

De gauche à droite, de haut en bas:
Couloir, détail de la façade, atrium.
Droite: Vue sur l'entrée.

CLINICAL CENTER OF THE CITY OF WOLFSBURG,
WOLFSBURG, GERMANY

RAUH DAMM STILLER PARTNERS
WITH KOLLER HEITMANN SCHÜTZ
ARCHITECTS

www.rdspartner.de
Client: City of Wolfsburg, Completion: 2005, Gross floor area: 189,376 sq. ft., Photos: Rainer Mader.

Left: West façade. Links: Westfassade. Gauche: Façade ouest. | Right: Site plan. Rechts: Lageplan. Droite: Plan du site.

The clinic forum is a four-story hall with a glass ceiling between the new building and the old clinic that serves as a meeting and exhibition area. On the ground and first floor the main corridors connect the new and the old building. Ambulances and visitors arrive on the ground floor, the examination and treatment areas are on the first floor. The lifts and stairways, medical care rooms, and the patient baths are in the center of the four upper floors. Lounges and patients' dining areas are located between the wards. The center of each ward contains the nurses' workplaces and the rooms for the medical staff.

Das Klinik-Forum ist eine viergeschossige, glasüberdeckte Halle, die als Fläche für Begegnungen und Ausstellungen dient. Im Erdgeschoss und ersten Obergeschoss verbindet die Magistrale Neubau und altes Klinikum. Im Erdgeschoss findet der Ambulanz- und Besucherverkehr statt, im ersten Obergeschoss liegen Untersuchungs- und Behandlungsbereiche. Im Zentrum der Obergeschosse befinden sich Aufzüge und Treppenhäuser, Versorgungsräume und Patientenbäder. Zwischen den Stationen liegen Aufenthalts- und Speiseräume für Patienten. Das Pflegezentrum jeder Station enthält Schwesterndienstplätze und Personalräume.

Le forum de la clinique est un bâtiment en verre de quatre étages qui sert aux rencontres et aux expositions. Il est relié à l'ancien bâtiment au niveau du rez-de-chaussée et du premier étage. L'accueil des visiteurs et les salles pour soins externes se trouvent au rez-de-chaussée, les salles de diagnostic et celles réservées aux patients hospitalisés étant situées au premier étage. Des escaliers et des ascenseurs desservent les autres niveaux, où se trouvent les locaux techniques, les salles d'hydrothérapie, les réfectoires et salles de séjour des patients, ainsi que les bureaux des infirmières et les locaux réservés au personnel.

Passage to new building. Übergang zum Neubau. Accès au nouveau bâtiment.

From left to right, from above to below:
Entrance area, meeting area, entrance, atrium.
Right: Garden for recreations.

Von links nach rechts, von oben nach unten:
Eingangsbereich, Aufenthaltsraum, Eingang, Atrium.
Rechts: Garten zur Erholung.

De gauche à droite, de haut en bas:
Accès principal, espace de réunion, entrée, atrium.
Droite: Jardin extérieur.

ANADOLU MEDICAL CENTER,
GEBZE, TURKEY

www.rees.com
Client: Anadolu Medical Center, **Completion:** 2006, **Gross floor area:** 500,000 sq. ft., **Photos:** Courtesy of Rees Associates.

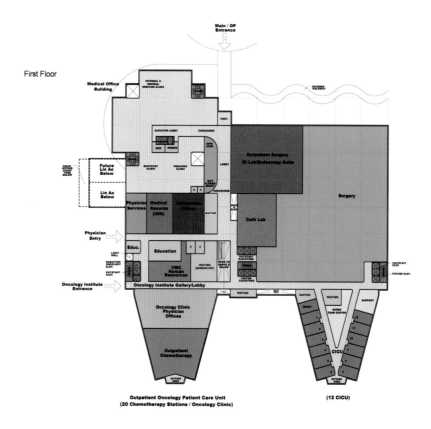

Left: Entrance view. Links: Ansicht vom Eingang. Gauche: Vue sur l'entrée. | Right: First floor plan. Rechts: Grundriss erste Etage. Droite: Plan du 1er étage.

The Anadolu Healthcare Village is Turkey's only hospital designed in line with the latest international healthcare standards. It will include a medical center with a hospital, rehabilitation center, medical office building, medical research institute, nursing college, hotel, nurses' residence, staff residence, assisted-living community, hospice, central services facility, village management center, and pharmacy. Completed in 2004, the first phase of the plan included the medical center, a medical office building, management offices and support facilities on an area of nearly 500,000 square feet.

Das Anadolu Healthcare Village ist die einzige Einrichtung in der Türkei, die den neuesten internationalen Standards der Krankenversorgung entspricht. Sie wird ein medizinisches Zentrum umfassen mit Krankenhaus, Rehabilitationszentrum, Ärztehaus, medizinischem Forschungsinstitut, Krankenpflegeschule, Hotel, Schwestern- und Mitarbeiterunterkünften, betreutem Wohnen, Hospiz, zentralen Serviceeinrichtungen, Verwaltungszentrum und Apotheke. Die 2004 abgeschlossene, erste Projektphase beinhaltete das medizinische Zentrum, ein Ärztehaus, Verwaltungsbüros und Versorgungseinrichtungen auf einer Fläche von fast 46.500 m².

Ce « village médicalisé » est le seul établissement hospitalier de Turquie à satisfaire aux standards internationaux en la matière. Il comprendra à terme un hôpital, une pharmacie, un centre de rééducation, un immeuble de bureaux, un institut de recherche, une résidence pour le personnel, une résidence médicalisée, un hôtel pour les familles des patients et divers bâtiments techniques et administratifs. La première phase de travaux, terminée en 2004, portait sur la réalisation de plus de 150 000 mètres carrés de locaux destinés au centre médical, à l'immeuble de bureaux et aux bâtiments techniques.

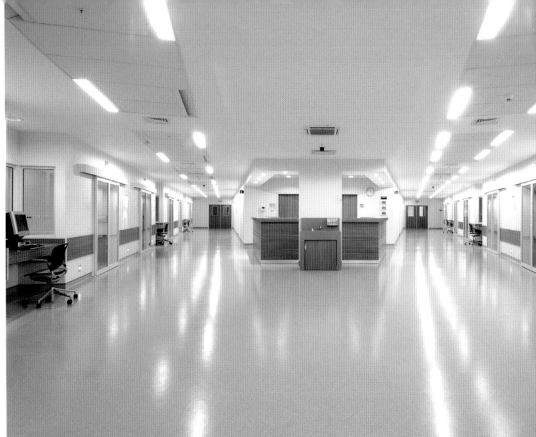

From left to right, from above to below:
Detail façade, ward track, nurse station, staircase.
Right: Entrance hall with reception area.

Von links nach rechts, von oben nach unten:
Fassadendetail, Stationsflur,
Schwesternarbeitsplatz, Treppenhaus.
Rechts: Eingangshalle mit Empfangsbereich.

De gauche à droite, de haut en bas:
Détail de la façade, couloirs,
bureau d'informations, escalier.
Droite: Hall d'entrée et espace d'accueil.

COMMUNITY HOSPITAL NORTH NEW WOMEN & INFANTS CENTER,
INDIANAPOLIS, IN, USA

RTKL ASSOCIATES INC.

www.rtkl.com
Client: Community Health Network. **Completion:** 2007. **Gross floor area:** 37,160 m². **Photos:** Jeffrey Totaro / Est.

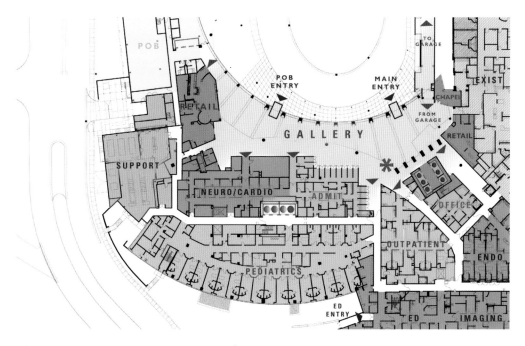

Left: Entrance area. Links: Eingangsbereich. Gauche: Entrée. | Right: Ground floor plan. Rechts: Grundriss Erdgeschoss. Droite: Plan du rez-de-chaussée.

The focal point of the expansion and renovation of Community Hospital North is a new 37,000 m², six-story tower that houses one of the largest and most advanced women's and children's hospitals in the US. Included within the facility are 60 single-room LDRP maternity suites, 36 private NICU suites and 20 private pediatric suites. Each of the new patient rooms will provide private zones for both the patient and his or her family. The entire project has been designed to enhance the patient and family healing experience with an environment intended to be comforting and elegant, including the same aesthetics found in four-star hotels.

Im Mittelpunkt der Erweiterung und des Umbaus des Community Hospital North steht ein neuer sechsge-schossiger Turm mit 37.000 m². Er beherbergt eine der größten und modernsten Frauen- und Kinder-kliniken der USA. Zu der Einrichtung gehören 60 Einbettzimmer der Entbindungsstation, 36 Intensiv-einheiten für Neugeborene und 20 Einzelzimmer für Kinder. Alle neuen Patientenräume verfügen über Pri-vatbereiche für den Patienten und seine Familie. Ziel des gesamten Projekts ist, den Genesungsprozess in einem wohligen und eleganten Umfeld mit der Ästhetik eines Vier-Sterne-Hotels zu fördern.

De récents travaux de rénovation et d'agrandisse-ment ont porté principalement sur la construction d'une tour de 37 000 m² sur six étages devant abriter l'hôpital pour femmes et enfants le plus grand et le plus moderne des États-Unis. On y trouve une maternité avec soixante chambres individuelles pour les mamans, trente-six chambres individuelles pour soins intensifs aux nouveaux-nées et vingt cham-bres individuelles pour enfants. Toutes les nouvelles chambres permettent aux patients de s'isoler avec leur famille. L'ensemble du projet vise à faciliter le processus de guérison grâce à un environnement réconfortant et agréable comparable à celui d'un hôtel quatre étoiles.

Rollins Family
Chapel

From left to right, from above to below:
Gallery at night, waiting area,
chapel entrance, entrance at night.
Right: Patient room.

Von links nach rechts, von oben nach unten:
Gallerie am Abend, Wartebereich,
Eingang zur Kapelle, Eingang am Abend.
Rechts: Patientenzimmer.

De gauche à droite, de haut en bas:
Galerie la nuit, salle d'attente,
entrée de la chapelle, vue sur l'entrée la nuit.
Droite: Chambre des patients.

WORKMEN'S COMPENSATION CASUALTY CLINIC,
LUDWIGSHAFEN / RHINE, GERMANY

SCHMUCKER AND PARTNERS PLANUNGSGESELLSCHAFT

www.schmucker-partner.de
Client: Verein für Berufsgenossenschaftliche Heilbehandlung Heidelberg e. V., **Completion:** 2005, **Gross floor area:** 560,058 sq. ft., **Photos:** Holger Schmidt.

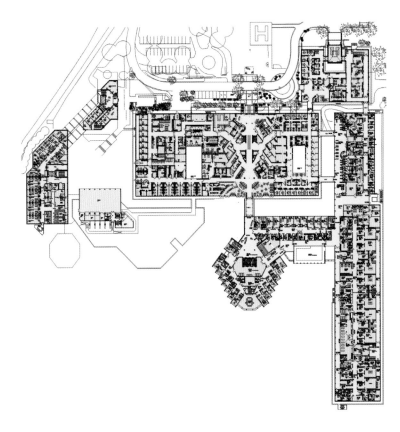

Left: **General view.** Links: **Gesamtansicht.** Gauche: Vue d'ensemble. | Right: **First floor plan.** Rechts: **Grundriss erste Etage.** Droite: Plan du 1er étage.

In the new tower the patients' rooms are arranged around an inner health care unit. An intermediate building links the operating theater wing and the ward tract tower. A large indoor swimming pool with two therapy pools and physiotherapy is located in the basement. There are ten new operating theaters, radiology and emergency admission across from the service floor and many areas were extended and converted. The entrance area on the ground floor, outpatient wards, accident and emergency departments, occupational therapy ward, three burn injury wards, and the cafeteria and kitchen area were redesigned.

Im neuen Bettenturm gruppieren sich die Patientenzimmer um einen Versorgungskern. Ein Zwischenbau mit Intensivstation verbindet den Turm mit dem neuen OP-Trakt. Im Funktionstrakt liegen zehn OPs, Radiologie sowie die Notfallaufnahme. Im Gartengeschoss sind die Physiotherapie und eine Schwimmhalle mit zwei Therapiebecken untergebracht. Zahlreiche Klinikbereiche wurden erweitert und umgebaut, so der Flachbau des Klinikhauptgebäudes. Hier fanden der Eingangsbereich sowie die Ambulanzen, Notaufnahme, Ergotherapie, drei Stationen für Brandverletzte und der Casino- und Küchenbereich eine neue Gestaltung.

Dans le nouveau bâtiment, les chambres des patients sont groupées autour d'un local de répartition. Une aile abritant les salles de soins intensifs relie la tour à la barre où se trouvent les dix salles d'opération, les urgences et la radiologique, ainsi que les services de physiothérapie qui sont dotés d'une piscine à deux bassins et situés au rez-de-chaussée côté jardin. Citons parmi les nombreux espaces agrandis et réaménagés le bâtiment qui abrite l'entrée, les cuisines, le restaurant, les services d'ergothérapie et les salles de soins aux brûlés.

From left to right, from above to below:
Waiting area, reception, auditorium.
Right: Entrance area.

Von links nach rechts, von oben nach unten:
Wartebereich, Anmeldung, Auditorium.
Rechts: Eingangsbereich.

De gauche à droite, de haut en bas:
Salle d'attente, réception, auditorium.
Droite: Hall d'entrée.

HEALTHCARE CENTER SEEKIRCHEN,
SEEKIRCHEN, GERMANY

SEHW ARCHITECTS

www.sehw.de
Client: GSWB Gemeinnützige Salzburger Wohnbau GmbH, **Completion:** 2008, **Gross floor area:** 11,000 m²,
Photos: Linus Lintner.

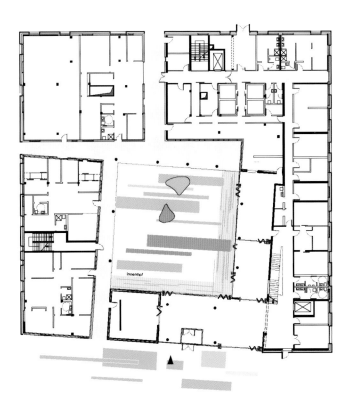

Left: Perforated façade. Links: Perforierte Fassade. Gauche: Façade perforée. | Right: Ground floor plan. Rechts: Grundriss Erdgeschoss. Droite: Plan du rez-de-chaussée.

Entrance to the building is from a forecourt through a generous foyer, which is used as a cafeteria at the same time. The foyer also provides a view of the central inner court, which serves as a leisure and central meeting point. A uniform outside cover provides a single image of the building despite its various uses inside. The façade consists of an inner thermal and structural physical layer and an outer layer that acts as weather protection, visual protection and sunscreen. The surface of the façade elements is perforated with pattern of leaves and foliage.

Von einem Vorplatz aus betritt man das Gebäude über ein großzügiges Foyer, das gleichzeitig als Cafeteria genutzt wird und in den zentralen Innenhof blicken lässt, der als Aufenthaltsort und zentraler Treffpunkt dient. Die unterschiedlichen Nutzungen im Inneren des Gebäudes werden nach Außen durch eine einheitliche Hülle zusammengefasst. Die Fassade besteht aus einer inneren, thermisch und bauphysikalisch relevanten Schicht und einer äußeren Schicht, die Witterungsschutz, Sichtschutz und Sonnenschutz übernimmt. Die Oberfläche der Fassadenelemente ist als Blatt- oder Laubmuster perforiert.

L'accès au bâtiment se fait par une esplanade et un vaste hall d'entrée qui abrite une cafétéria et donne sur la cour intérieure, véritable point de ralliement de ce centre médical. L'enveloppe du bâtiment unifie les différents espaces. Elle se compose d'une couche intérieure portante et isolante, doublée d'une couche extérieure qui protège des intempéries et du rayonnement solaire. Les perforations de la façade sont en forme de feuilles.

From left to right, from above to below:
Meeting room, ward and staircase,
balcony, staircase with skylight.
Right: Ward track.

Von links nach rechts, von oben nach unten:
Aufenthaltsraum, Station und Treppenhaus,
Balkon, Treppenhaus mit Oberlicht.
Rechts: Stationsflur.

De gauche à droite, de haut en bas:
Espace d'accueil, escaliers reliant les services,
balcon, escalier et plafond vitré.
Droite: Couloir d'un service.

KINGS COUNTY HOSPITAL CENTER,
BROOKLYN, NY, USA

SKIDMORE, OWINGS & MERRILL

www.som.com
Client: Dormitory Authority of the State of New York, **Completion:** 2006, **Gross floor area:** 57,600 sq. ft., **Photos:** Eduard Hueber, Archphoto.

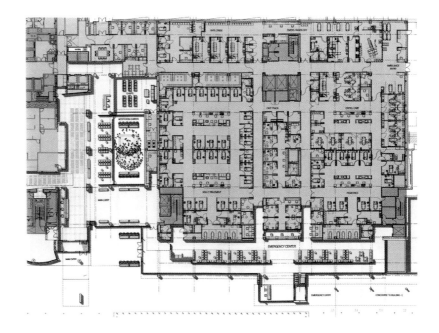

Left: Emergency entrance. Links: Notaufnahme. Gauche: Entrée des urgences. | Right: First floor plan. Rechts: Grundriss erste Etage. Droite: Plan du 1er étage.

SOM was charged with rehabilitating an early 20th-century hospital campus to function at a 21st-century level with $500 million. Phase One, the Inpatient Center, provides 340 beds, private and semi-private rooms, private bathrooms, and intensive care suites. Phase Two combined diagnostic and treatment services previously scattered among five or six buildings, including a 40,000-square-feet emergency room for adults and children. Phase Three was the renovation of an architecturally significant 1948 building to accommodate outpatient services, with examination, procedure and counseling rooms.

SOM erhielt den Auftrag, eine Krankenhausanlage aus dem frühen 20. Jahrhundert auf den Stand des 21. Jahrhunderts zu bringen. In der ersten Sanierungsphase stellte das Inpatient Center 340 Betten, private und halbprivate Räume, private Badezimmer und Intensiveinheiten bereit. Phase zwei fasste die zuvor auf fünf oder sechs Gebäude verteilten Diagnostik- und Behandlungseinrichtungen zusammen, darunter eine 3 716 m_ große Notaufnahme für Erwachsene und Kinder. Phase drei betraf den Umbau eines architektonisch bedeutenden Bauwerks aus dem Jahre 1948 zur Unterbringung von ambulanten Untersuchungs-, Behandlungs- und Beratungsräumen.

Le bureau SOM a été chargé de réhabiliter, pour la somme de 500 millions de dollars, cet hôpital construit au début du XXe siècle. La phase 1 visait à la réalisation de chambres individuelles et semi-individuelles de 340 lits au total, de salles de bain pour les patients et d'une unité de soins intensifs. La phase 2 a porté sur le regroupement des services de consultation et de soins auparavant dispersés dans une demi-douzaine de bâtiments, et sur la modernisation d'une salle d'urgence de 12 000 mètres carrés pour enfants et adultes. Quant à la phase 3, elle consistait en la rénovation d'un bâtiment datant de 1948 qui abrite désormais les salles de consultation, de soins et de conseil destinées aux patients externes.

Aerial view. Luftbild. Vue aérienne.

From left to right, from above to below:
Entrance, reception, waiting area.
Right: Reception area.

Von links nach rechts, von oben nach unten:
Eingang, Empfang, Wartebereich.
Rechts: Empfangsbereich.

De gauche à droite, de haut en bas:
Entrée, réception, salle d'attente.
Droite: Espace de réception.

NEW MESTRE HOSPITAL,
VENETO, ITALY

STUDIO ALTIERI S.P.A

www.studioaltieri.it

Client: Azienda ULSS12 Venezian, **Completion:** 2008, **Gross floor area:** 113,829 m², **Photos:** Studio Altieri, studio Maggi/ Moreno Magg.

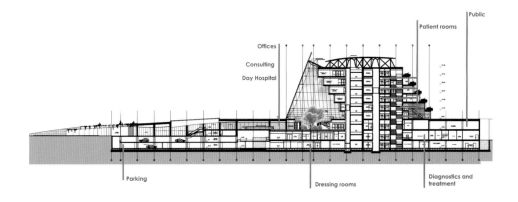

Left: **Exterior view.** Links: **Außenansicht.** Gauche: Vue extérieure. | Right: **Section.** Rechts: Schnitt. Droite: Coupe.

The main building is composed of two separate parts – the technological platform area and the in-patient room block. This block contains a three-floor platform area and seven floors above ground, five of which accommodate hospitalized patients. The platform area is a reinforced concrete construction; the single "residential" block construction on top is a mix of steel and concrete. A large sail-shaped glass structure the same height as the building links the two parts, stretching along the length of the building and covering a spacious, bright entrance hall linked to all facilities and contact areas.

Das Hauptgebäude setzt sich aus zwei separaten Teilen zusammen – der Plattenkonstruktion mit dem Technikbereich und dem Bettenhaus. Das Bettenhaus besteht aus einer dreigeschossigen Plattenkonstruktion und sieben Ebenen darüber, von denen fünf für stationäre Patienten bestimmt sind. Die Plattenkonstruktion ist ein Stahlbetonbau; der ihm aufgesetzte „Wohn"-Block kombiniert Stahl und Beton. Ein gleich hoher segelförmiger Glasbau verbindet die beiden Teile miteinander. Er erstreckt sich über die gesamte Gebäudelänge und überdacht eine weitläufige, helle Eingangshalle, die alle Einrichtungen und Kontaktbereiche erschließt.

Le bâtiment principal se compose de deux entités distinctes : la plate-forme technologique et l'immeuble abritant les chambres des patients. Ce dernier inclut trois niveaux souterrains en béton armé et sept niveaux à l'air libre en béton et acier, dont cinq réservés aux chambres. Une gigantesque structure en verre en forme de voile unifie les deux entités. Elle s'étire tout au long du bâtiment et couvre un vaste hall d'entrée qui donne accès à tous les services de l'hôpital.

Fully glazed façade. Komplett verglaste Fassade. Façade entièrement vitrée.

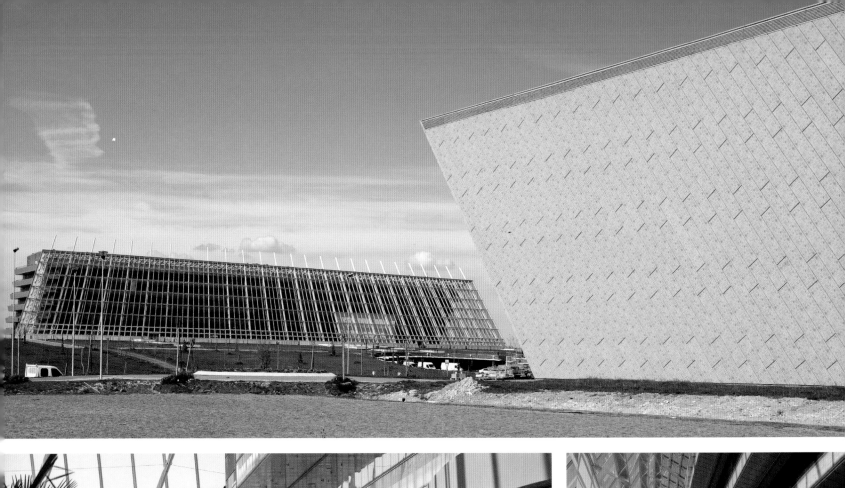

From left to right, from above to below:
General view, entrance hall, glazed ceiling.
Right: Entrance view.

Von links nach rechts, von oben nach unten:
Gesamtansicht, Eingangshalle, verglaste Decke.
Rechts: Ansicht vom Eingang.

De gauche à droite, de haut en bas:
Vue d'ensemble, hall d'entrée, plafond vitré.
Droite: Vue sur l'entrée.

CATHOLIC HOSPITAL OF ST. JOHANN NEPOMUK,
ERFURT, GERMANY

TMK ARCHITECTS · ENGINEERS

www.tmk-architekten.de

Client: St. Johann Nepomuk Foundation, Completion: 2003, Gross floor area: 462,680 sq. ft., Photos: Jochen Stüber, Object Photography.

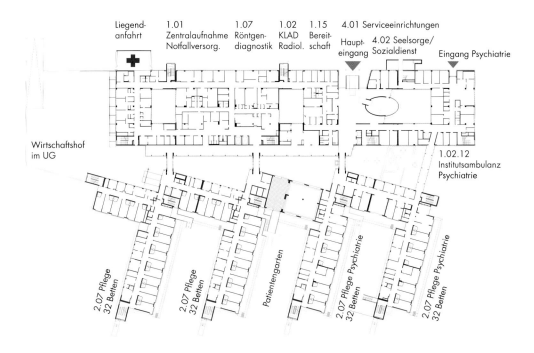

Left: Entrance chapel. Links: Eingang zur Kapelle. Gauche: Entrée de la chapelle. | Right: Ground floor plan. Rechts: Grundriss Erdgeschoss. Droite: Plan du rez-de-chaussée.

Each floor contains four wards designed for 32 beds. A four-story glazed corridor links the two buildings. The central admission point with emergency medical care and radiological diagnostics units is located on the ground floor. The specialist outpatient clinics are situated next to the main entrance with an integrated chapel and cafeteria. All medical services are located on the first floor to the right of the two-story entrance hall and the outpatient psychiatry clinic. The second floor contains operating theaters, an intensive care ward, a central sterilization department, and a maternity ward.

Jede Ebene nimmt vier Stationen für jeweils 32 Betten auf. Ein viergeschossiger gläserner Korridor verbindet die zwei Bauten miteinander. Im Erdgeschoss befinden sich die Eingangshalle mit dem Empfang, die Notaufnahme und das Institut für bildgebende Diagnostik. Neben dem Haupteingang mit integrierter Kapelle und Cafeteria liegen die verschiedenen Tageskliniken. Der gesamte klinische Arztdienst ist in der ersten Ebene rechts neben der zweigeschossigen Eingangshalle und der Tagesklinik der Psychiatrie untergebracht. Die zweite Ebene verfügt über Operationssäle sowie die Abteilungen Zentralsterilisation und Geburtshilfe.

Quatre salles de soins de trente-deux lits se trouvent à chaque étage. Une aile en verre de quatre étages relie les deux bâtiments du complexe. Les urgences et la radiologie sont situées au rez-de-chaussée. Les salles de consultation externes, complétées par une cafétéria et une chapelle, se trouvent près de l'entrée principale. Tous les autres services médicaux se concentrent au premier étage, à droite du hall d'accès sur deux niveaux et de la clinique psychiatrique pour patients externes. Au second étage, on trouve une maternité, des blocs opératoires, une salle de soins intensifs et une unité de stérilisation centralisée.

From left to right, from above to below:
South façade, detail façade, entrance view.
Right: Patients garden.

Von links nach rechts, von oben nach unten:
Südfassade, Fassadendetail, Eingangsansicht.
Rechts: Patientengarten.

De gauche à droite, de haut en bas:
Façade sud, détail de la façade, vue sur l'entrée.
Droite: Jardin pour les patients.

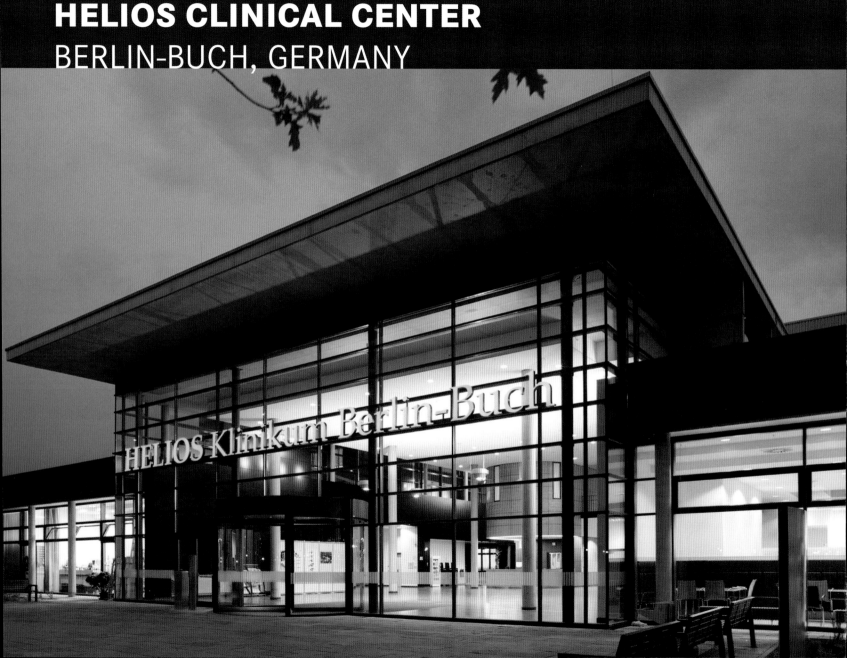

TMK ARCHITECTS · ENGINEERS

www.tmk-architekten.de
Client: Helios Klininiken GmbH, **Completion:** 2006, **Gross floor area:** 968,400 sq. ft., **Photos:** Linus Lintner, Berlin.

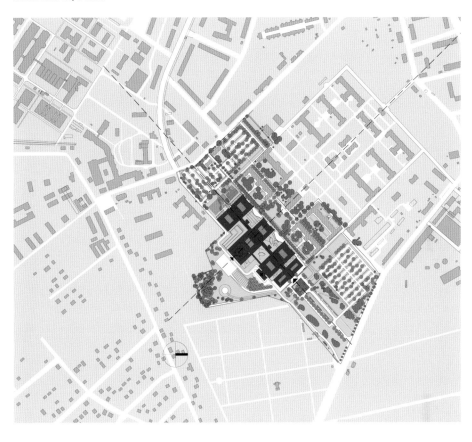

Left: **Main entrance.** Links: Haupteingang. Gauche: Entrée principale. | Right: **Site plan.** Rechts: Lageplan. Droite: Plan du site.

The style of the new buildings is based on the listed original building. Five square bedroom buildings were constructed with a compact design with large central atriums. The operating center to the south of the premises is directly connected to the buildings by a passageway. The ground floor of the four buildings is reserved to the various examination, diagnosis and treatment offers. Short paths link the buildings supporting their multi-functionality. The two main avenues meet axially in the large five-story conference towers of the new building, who lean on the glass passageway.

Die Neubauten orientieren sich am denkmalgeschützten Altbestand. In kompakter Typologie entstanden fünf quadratische Bettenhäuser, deren Mittelpunkt große Atrien bilden. Das OP-Zentrum im Süden der Anlage schließt sich über eine Magistrale direkt an die Bettenhäuser an. Die Erdgeschosse aller Baukörper sind den vielfältigen Untersuchungs-, Diagnostik- und Behandlungsangeboten vorbehalten. Kurze Wege verbinden die Baublöcke im Sinne der Multifunktionalität. Die beiden Hauptalleen münden axial in den großen Konferenztürmen des Neubaus, die fünfgeschossig an die gläserne Magistrale angelehnt sind.

Cinq nouveaux bâtiments groupés autour de cours intérieures sous verrières s'inspirent des édifices préexistants classés monuments historiques. Une grande allée relie les bâtiments abritant les chambres au bâtiment des blocs opératoires, situé au sud du complexe. Des salles de soins et de diagnostic se trouvent au rez-de-chaussée de tous les nouveaux bâtiments. Les architectes ont cherché à minimiser les déplacements à l'intérieur du complexe. Les deux allées principales sont dans l'axe de la salle de conférence du nouveau bâtiment de cinq étages.

From left to right, from above to below:
Meeting area nursing station, atrium, entrance hall, hallway.
Right: Exterior view center line.

Von links nach rechts, von oben nach unten:
Aufenthaltsbereich Pflegestation, Atrium, Eingangshalle, Flur.
Rechts: Außenansicht Magistrale.

De gauche à droite, de haut en bas:
Espace d'accueil, atrium, hall d'entrée, couloir.
Droite: Vue extérieure sur le bâtiment.

JOHANNES WESLING CLINICAL CENTER,
MINDEN, GERMANY

www.tmk-architekten.de
Client: Zweckverband der Kliniken im Mühlenkreis, Completion: 2008, Gross floor area: 98,000 m²,
Photos: Jochen Stüber, Hamburg.

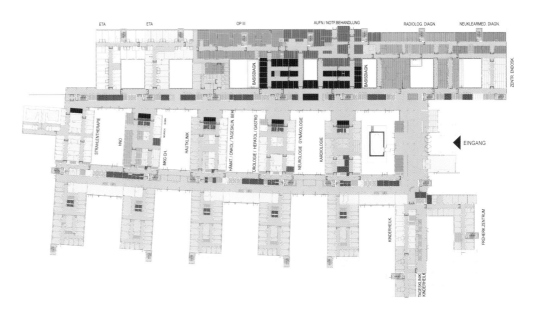

Left: Main entrance. Links: Haupteingang. Gauche: Entrée principale. | Right: Ground floor plan. Rechts: Grundriss Erdgeschoss. Droite: Plan du rez-de-chaussée.

Across a floor space of 46,000 m², three to four floors contain a total of 864 beds and 18 operating theaters. The core of the hospital is a 300-meter-long reception, diagnosis and therapy section, which stretches across the entire length of the building. The areas for visitors and patients separate in the entry section. While patients use the northern passageway to reach all examination and treatment rooms, visitors use the southern passageway for direct access to the stations.

Auf einer Nutzfläche von 46.000 m² finden sich auf drei bis vier Geschossen insgesamt über 864 Betten und 18 OP-Säle. Kernstück des Klinikums ist der 300 Meter lange Aufnahme-, Diagnostik- und Therapietrakt, der sich über die gesamte Gebäudelänge zieht. Die Wege von Patienten und Besuchern trennen sich vom Eingangsbereich an. Während die Patienten die Nordmagistrale nutzen und über diesen Weg alle Untersuchungs- und Behandlungsräume erreichen, nutzen die Besucher die Südmagistrale als direkten Zugang zu den Stationen.

Cet hôpital d'une surface totale de 46 000 m² répartis entre plusieurs immeubles de trois et quatre étages regroupe dix-huit salles d'opération et 864 lits. Au cœur du complexe se trouve un bâtiment d'environ trois cents mètres de long qui abrite les services administratifs et les salles de diagnostic et de traitement. Deux itinéraires distincts sont possibles à partir du hall d'entrée : le couloir qui part vers le nord dessert les espaces réservés aux patients venant bénéficier de soins externes, tandis que le couloir sud mène directement aux chambres des patients hospitalisés.

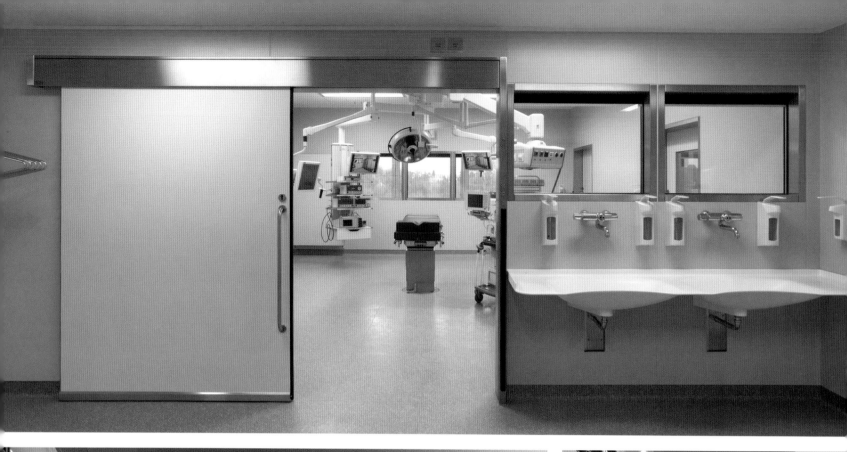

From left to right, from above to below:
Operating theater, hallway, cafeteria.
Right: Terrace in courtyard.

Von links nach rechts, von oben nach unten:
OP-Bereich, Halle, Cafeteria.
Rechts: Außenterasse.

De gauche à droite, de haut en bas:
Salle des opérations, couloir, cafétéria.
Droite: Terrasse extérieure.

FLETCHER ALLEN HEALTH CARE, THE RENAISSANCE PROJECT,
BURLINGTON, VT, USA

www.tka-architects.com
Client: Fletcher Allen Health Care, **Completion:** 2005, **Gross floor area:** 88,258 m², **Photos:** Robert Beson, Hartford, CT (280, 282a.r., 282 b.r., 282 b.l., 283), Peter Mauss/Esto, Marmaroneck, NY (282 a.l.).

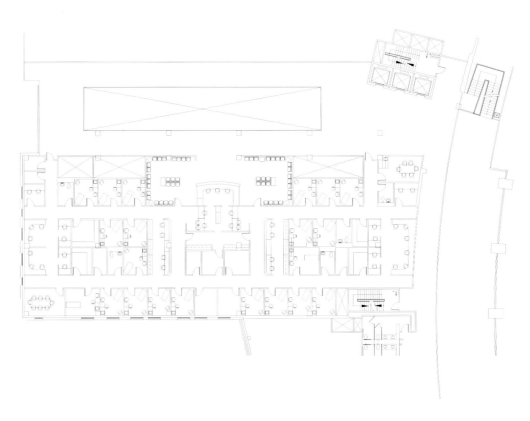

Left: Entrance. Links: Eingang. Gauche: Entrée. | Right: Floor plan. Rechts: Grundriss. Droite: Plan.

This healthcare building represents the first phase of a three-part master plan to unite clinical, education, and research efforts on Fletcher Allen Health Care's main campus. This phase integrates an ambulatory care center, a medical education center and library, a central utilities plant, and an underground parking structure designed with a landscaped roof that provides a formal street-level approach to the main pavilion. Project goals included establishing a clear sense of place, improving access through a single point of entry, and creating a meaningful connection with the natural environment.

Das Krankenhausgebäude repräsentiert die erste Phase eines dreiteiligen Masterplans, der die Bereiche Klinik, Ausbildung und Forschung auf dem Hauptcampus der Fletcher Allen Poliklinik vereint. Es umfasst eine Ambulanz, ein medizinisches Ausbildungszentrum mit Bibliothek sowie zentrale Versorgungseinrichtungen. Über das landschaftlich gestaltete Dach der Tiefgarage gelangt man auf Straßenniveau zum Hauptpavillon. Die Projektziele beinhalteten die Entwicklung eines eindeutigen Gefühls für den Ort, eine bessere Erschließung durch einen einzigen Eingangsbereich und die harmonische Einbindung in das natürliche Umfeld.

La réalisation de ce bâtiment constitue la première partie d'un plan en trois phases visant à unifier les services de soins, de formation et de recherche sur le campus Fletcher Allen Health Care. Ce CHU abrite un centre de soins pour patients externes, une unité de services centralisés, une bibliothèque, des salles de cours et un parking souterrain dont le plafond décoré assure la transition avec la rue. Le cahier des charges exigeait une organisation spatiale claire, une entrée centralisée et une intégration des bâtiments à l'environnement naturel.

From left to right, from above to below:
Meeting area first floor,
view to atrium, waiting area, atrium.
Right: Planted courtyard

Von links nach rechts, von oben nach unten:
Aufenthaltsbereich erste Etage,
Blick ins Atrium, Wartebereich, Atrium.
Bepflanzter Innenhof.

De gauche à droite, de haut en bas:
Salle d'accueil au 1er étage,
vue sur l'atrium, salle d'attente, atrium.
Droite: Cour extérieure arborée.

THE CHILDREN'S HOSPITAL,
PORTLAND, OR, USA

ZIMMER GUNSUL FRASCA ARCHITECTS

www.zgf.com

Client: The Children's Hospital, **Completion:** 2007, **Gross floor area:** 133,780 m², **Photos:** © Eckert & Eckert / Portland, Oregon USA.

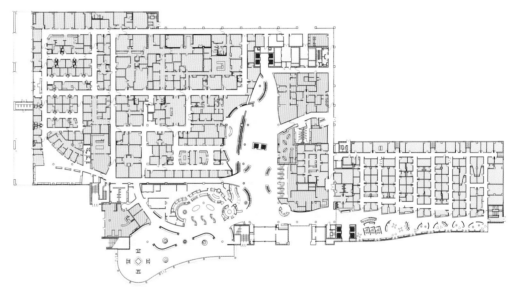

Left: Waiting area. Links: Wartebereich. Gauche: Salle d'attente. | Right: First floor plan. Rechts: Grundriss erste Etage. Droite: Plan du 1er étage.

When The Children's Hospital set out to build its new $425 million facility, the mission was straightforward: create the most healing hospital for kids by embodying both the concept of family-centered care and utilizing the latest evidence-based design techniques. The result is a 1.44 million square-feet hospital that is bright, nurturing, calm and full of amenities – from a gelato bar, to a teen "hot spot" featuring a movie theater and pool table, to staff and patient lounges.

Bei der Planung einer neuen, 425 Millionen Dollar teuren Einrichtung für The Children's Hospital waren die Vorgaben einfach: ein sehr effizientes Kinderkrankenhaus durch die Einbeziehung eines familienorientierten Behandlungskonzepts und die Verwendung modernster empirischer Entwurfsmethoden. Das Ergebnis ist eine Klinik mit einer Fläche von 133.780 m². Sie zeichnet sich durch eine helle, fröhliche und ruhige Atmosphäre aus und besitzt viele Annehmlichkeiten – wie eine Gelato-Bar über einen Teenager-„Hotspot" mit Kino und Billardtisch bis zu den Sitzgelegenheiten für Mitarbeiter und Patienten.

L'objectif était clair lors du lancement de ce projet de 425 millions de dollars : optimiser les soins destinés aux enfants grâce à un concept reprenant les structures familiales et à l'utilisation des toutes dernières techniques architecturales. Les travaux ont eu pour résultat un hôpital clair, calme, réconfortant et pourvu de divers agréments, notamment un café glacier, des salles de détente pour les patients et le personnel, ainsi qu'un espace pour les ados avec cinéma et billard.

General view. Gesamtansicht. Vue d'ensemble.

From left to right, from above to below:
Exterior seating, cafeteria, nurse station, atrium.
Right: Nurse station.

Von links nach rechts, von oben nach unten:
Außenliegende Sitzgelegenheit, Cafeteria,
Schwesternarbeitsplatz, Atrium.
Rechts: Schwesternarbeitsplatz.

De gauche à droite, de haut en bas:
Terrasse extérieure, cafétéria,
espace de travail des infirmières, atrium.
Droite: Espace des infirmières.

LEGACY SALMON CREEK HOSPITAL,
PORTLAND, OR, USA

ZIMMER GUNSUL FRASCA
ARCHITECTS

www.zgf.com
Client: Legacy Health System, Portland, Oregon, **Completion:** 2006, **Gross floor area:** 43,571 m², **Photos:** © Eckert & Eckert, © Robert Canfield Photography.

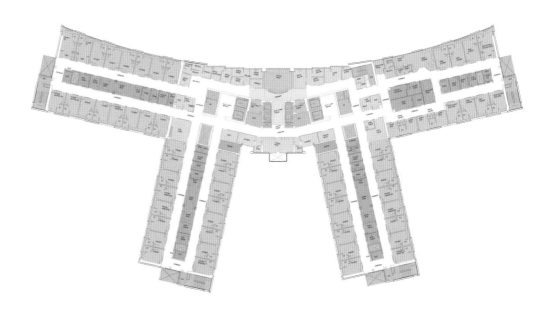

Left: Pedestrian bridge. Links: Fußgängerbrücke. Gauche: Tunnel reliant les services. | Right: Fifth floor plan. Rechts: Grundriss fünfte Etage. Droite: Plan du 5e étage.

The 1,124,000 square-feet facility features a six-story bed tower, two four story medical office buildings with a connecting atrium, and a seven-story parking structure with space for 1,464 vehicles. The 220-bed hospital includes a 16-bed ICU, 16 step-down beds and 15 NICU beds. There are 10 major operating rooms, three endoscopy operating rooms and two catheterization labs. Cancer services are provided primarily on an outpatient basis in the first medical office building. A 10,000 square-feet radiation oncology suite with two linear accelerators and a CT/simulator is housed on the first floor of the medical office building.

Die 104.423 m² große Einrichtung beinhaltet einen sechsgeschossigen Bettenturm, zwei viergeschossige Ärztehäuser mit einem dazwischenliegenden Atrium und ein Parkhaus mit sieben Ebenen für 1.464 Fahrzeuge. Das 220-Betten-Krankenhaus verfügt über eine Intensivstation mit 16 Betten, 16 Nachsorgebetten und 15 Plätze auf der Neugeborenen-Intensivstation. Vorhanden sind 10 Operationssäle, drei Endoskopieräume und zwei Katheterlabore. Krebspatienten werden hauptsächlich in der Tagesklinik im ersten Ärztehaus versorgt. Eine 929 m² große Radioonkologie mit zwei Linearbeschleunigern und einem Computertomografen befindet sich auf der ersten Etage des Ärztehauses.

Cet ensemble de 350 000 mètres carrés se compose d'une tour de six étages abritant les chambres des patients, de deux immeubles administratifs de quatre étages reliés par une verrière et d'un garage sur sept niveaux avec 1464 places de parking. Il compte 220 lits au total, dont seize pour soins intensifs, quinze pour soins intensifs aux nouveau-nés et seize lits mobiles. On y trouve dix salles d'opération généralistes, trois salles d'opération pour endoscopie et deux laboratoires de cathétérisation. Un bâtiment est réservé aux soins externes prodigués aux cancéreux, avec au premier étage une salle de radiation équipée de deux accélérateurs linéaires et d'un simulateur CT.

Overall front face from garden. Gesamtansicht aus dem Garten. Vue d'ensemble depuis le jardin.

From left to right, from above to below:
Second floor of main lobby, patient room,
intensive care unit waiting room.
Right: Interior courtyard.

Von links nach rechts, von oben nach unten:
Hauptlobby zweite Etage, Patientenzimmer,
Wartezimmer Intensivstation.
Rechts: Innenhof.

De gauche à droite, de haut en bas:
Hall au 2e étage, chambre des patients,
salle d'attente des soins intensifs.
Droite: Cour intérieure.

REBECCA AND JOHN MOORES UCSD CANCER CENTER,
SAN DIEGO, CA, USA

ZIMMER GUNSUL FRASCA
ARCHITECTS

www.zgf.com

Client: University of California, San Diego, **Completion:** 2005, **Gross floor area:** 25,083 m², **Photos:**
© Nick Merrick / Hedrich Blessing, © Robert Canfield.

Left: **Front view along clinic.** Links: Vorderansicht. Gauche: Vue frontale de la clinique. | Right: **Second floor plan.** Rechts: Grundriss zweite Etage. Droite: Plan du 2e étage.

The facility required space for clinical care, basic research, cancer prevention and control, and administration departments. The plan was to bring researchers, clinicians, prevention specialists and educators under one roof in a "bench-to-bedside" approach to conquering cancer. The clinical care component includes exam and procedure rooms, chemotherapy, radiation oncology, chemotherapy/infusion, imaging, physician offices, and support spaces. The Cancer Prevention and Control program includes administrative space for clinical trials, community outreach and cancer prevention education programs.

Die Einrichtung benötigte Raum für die klinische Versorgung, Grundlagenforschung, Krebsprävention und –kontrolle sowie für Verwaltungsabteilungen. Im Kampf gegen den Krebs sollten Forscher, Krankenhausärzte, Präventionsspezialisten und Pädagogen unter einem Dach zusammenkommen. Zum Klinikbereich gehören Untersuchungs- und Behandlungsräume, Chemotherapie, Radioonkologie, Chemotherapie/Infusion, Bildverarbeitung, Arztzimmer und Versorgungsräume. Das Programm zur Krebsprävention und –kontrolle beinhaltet Verwaltungsbüros für klinische Studien, die Unterstützung von Betroffenen und Aufklärungsprogramme zur Krebsvorbeugung.

L'hôpital avait besoin de plus de place pour les soins, la recherche fondamentale, la prévention du cancer et les services administratifs. L'idée retenue pour les travaux d'agrandissement consiste à rassembler sous le même toit les chercheurs, les médecins, les enseignants et les spécialistes de la prévention afin de mieux lutter contre le cancer. Les espaces cliniques incluent des salles de consultation et de soins ainsi que des salles de chimiothérapie, de radiation, d'infusion et d'imagerie médicale, auxquelles s'ajoutent les cabinets des médecins et les espaces annexes. Le programme national de prévention et de contrôle du cancer prévoit des espaces pour les tests cliniques, les travaux de proximité et la pédagogie de la prévention du cancer.

Entrance at night. Eingang am Abend. Entrée de nuit.

From left to right, from above to below:
Meeting area, interior,
infusion center waiting room, bamboo courtyard.
Right: View of lobby.

Von links nach rechts, von oben nach unten:
Aufenthaltsraum, Innenansicht,
Warteraum Infusionszimmer, Innenhof mit Bambus.
Rechts: Ansicht der Lobby.

De gauche à droite, de haut en bas:
Salle de rencontre, intérieur, salle d'attente du service
des perfusions, cour intérieure avec bambous.
Droite: Vue sur le hall d'accueil.

INDEX.

Imprint

The Deutsche Bibliothek is registering this publication in the Deutsche Na-
tionalbibliographie; detailed bibliographical information can be found on the
internet at http://dnb.ddb.de

ISBN 978-3-03768-006-3

© 2009 by Braun Publishing AG

1st edition 2009

Project coordinator: Annika Schulz
Editorial staff: Dagmar Glück
Translation: Claire Chamot, Marcel Saché, Cosima Talhouni,
Joanna Zajac-Heinken
Lektorat: Cosima Talhouni
Graphic concept and layout: Michaela Prinz